The Book of Esther

John J Sweetman

Copyright January 2021

All Scripture references are from the New Living Translation of the Bible except when stated otherwise.

Introduction

This account of Esther is unusual in two respects. First, it is the only book of the Old Testament which does not mention God. Despite that apparent attempt to remain hidden, God's involvement behind the scenes becomes increasingly evident as the story of Esther is played out. Secondly, it is one of only two books named after a woman, the other being Ruth.

It is written anonymously, although both Ezra and Mordecai have been suggested as possible authors. Over the years, others have added extra details to the story of Esther, often including the name of God. These additions are not generally accepted as being authentic but have been inserted into the Apocrypha.

Esther is the story of a poor but beautiful Jewish girl who becomes the wife of King Xerxes, ruler of the Medes and Persians Empire and the most powerful king in the world. In that position of responsibility, Esther and her older cousin, Mordecai, are able to save the nation of Israel from a plot to exterminate them throughout the empire. The involvement of God can be seen in the many "coincidences" which had to occur for the nation to be saved.

There are many similarities in the story of Esther with that of Joseph in Genesis. In both situations God positions a person of no value by the world's standards into a position of power in order to outwork His purposes for His people.

By the time Esther was born, the Babylonian empire had fallen to the Medes and Persians. Babylon was no longer the only centre of an empire. That honour was shared between several major cities, one of them being Susa where King Xerxes reigned during the events written about in Esther between BC 483-473. Several years earlier, Sheshbazzar, with Ezra and 50,000 exiles, had returned to rebuild the Temple in Jerusalem in BC 538. But many Jews had decided to remain in captivity, including Esther's forebears. The walls around Jerusalem would not be rebuilt until BC 445.

Whilst a comparatively small community of Jews were focussed on rebuilding Jerusalem, the majority of Israel remained in captivity preferring to devote their time towards building wealth and security for themselves throughout the Empire. This is a similar picture to Christians today. A small remnant is devoting their lives to establishing the Kingdom of God whilst the majority are content to invest their time and energy in ensuring wealth and security in the world.

However, although we might seek peace and security, we have an enemy, Satan, who plans to destroy God's people. This book of Esther helps us to understand how that plan will be set in motion. After the temple in Jerusalem was rebuilt and before the walls of the city could be fortified, Satan sought to destroy all Israel. It will be the same for us today. After we have found harmony in the Church there will be a time of great harvest. But during that time, the plans of Satan will need to be exposed and brought to nothing.

The Persian Empire was near its peak during Xerxes' reign. Many major nations had been conquered including Egypt. And the wealth from the taxation of these nations poured into the Persian capital of Susa, enabling Xerxes to build a luxurious new palace at Persepolis. We can compare this new palace with the temple in Jerusalem. The palace was built with forced labour and from the wealth gained through overcoming and controlling nations through war. The temple was built through voluntary hard work and meagre resources.

The book of Esther was written to confirm to Israel that despite their exile they were still the chosen nation of God. It also had the consequence of showing how God is able to preserve His chosen remnant wherever they lived in the world. God was not limited to saving His people in the specific geographic area of Israel.

There is considerable prophetic symbolism throughout this story of Esther. Although the events occurred many years before the birth of Jesus, they have power to speak to us about our own generation.

One

Esther 1:1-6 *"These events happened in the days of King Xerxes, who reigned over 127 provinces stretching from India to Ethiopia. At that time Xerxes ruled his empire from his royal throne at the fortress of Susa. In the third year of his reign, he gave a banquet for all his nobles and officials. He invited all the military officers of Persia and Media as well as the princes and nobles of the provinces. The celebration lasted 180 days—a tremendous display of the opulent wealth of his empire and the pomp and splendour of his majesty. When it was all over, the king gave a banquet for all the people, from the greatest to the least, who were in the fortress of Susa. It lasted for seven days and was held in the courtyard of the palace garden. The courtyard was beautifully decorated with white cotton curtains and blue hangings, which were fastened with white linen cords and purple ribbons to silver rings embedded in marble pillars. Gold and silver couches stood on a mosaic pavement of porphyry, marble, mother-of-pearl, and other costly stones."*

King Xerxes, otherwise known as Ahasuerus, was son of Darius I (521–486 BC), who was king when Haggai and Zechariah encouraged the people of Judah to finish building the Temple in Jerusalem. Xerxes was a ruthless king who reigned over a vast empire stretching from India to Ethiopia. He reigned between 486-465 BC.

Susa, located in modern day Iran, was the winter residence of the king. It was one of Persia's four capital cities (Neh. 1:1; Dan. 8:2). The three other capitals were Ecbatana (Ezr 6:2), Babylon and Persepolis. One of Daniel's visions was set in Susa (Da 8:2); Nehemiah also served there (Ne 1:1). Media was in Northwestern Persia, near the Caspian Sea. Although once a separate nation, it was conquered c. 550 B.C. by Cyrus the Great, who founded the Persian Empire.

As the military did not normally fight during the winter months, Xerxes arranged a lavish festival for 180 days to maintain the morale of his army and to exhibit his vast wealth. As many nobles and military personnel from throughout the Empire were invited to the festival, it is unlikely that everyone was present throughout. It is more likely that the king held different events and feasts each day to demonstrate his military force and wealth. Today, a nation would display its military capability by parading the army and artillery with a march past the President each day. King Xerxes is likely to have promoted his power in a similar way.

When the festival came to an end the king gave a feast to everyone in Susa which lasted for seven days. Again, it is unlikely that everyone came to each meal provided as the palace grounds would not have been large enough to hold so many people.

We are told that the hangings, fixtures and fittings were exquisite and expensive. It is difficult to imagine what the people thought when they were invited to feast in a place and with food which was so different from their normal fare.

The reason for the king's apparent generosity was his pride. Xerxes did not put on a display of wealth in order to bless his people by feeding them. He was a ruthless tyrant without genuine love. His motive was to show anyone who might want to overthrow him that he had the support of a mighty army and the ability to buy as much help as needed.

However, the purpose of the book of Esther is not to glorify a tyrannical king. Xerxes might be a key player in the drama but his power and wealth are insignificant in the final outcome. There is a much greater purpose in the book to show that God's plans and purposes will prevail despite what man seeks to achieve.

Today, throughout the world, there are many powerful and wealthy people, such as governments, who are able to control vast numbers of citizens. Those who control might be democratically elected but others are not. The majority of those people who are being controlled are poor and feel unable to do anything to change their situation. The election process, where there is one, is often flawed. And unelected leaders do not always act in the best interests of the citizens of the country.

It is not only the governments which control people. A direct consequence of the rebellion of Adam and Eve against God in the Garden of Eden was that they surrendered authority to Satan setting in motion the spiritual law that husbands and wives would seek to control each other (Genesis 3:16). The fact is that individuals seek to control others. Sadly, that desire to control is often found within the Church system. Despite the fact that there is universal control of others, the book of Esther gives us hope that God is able to turn any impossible situation on its head.

As we study Esther we will find that the Jews faced extermination because of the edicts of Xerxes; edicts passed after the manipulation of Haman. There comes a time in most people's life when we face impossible situations. The experience of Esther and Mordecai helps us to find God in those times. We find hope replaces despair as we trust in what He can do.

Two

Esther 1:7-9 *"Drinks were served in gold goblets of many designs, and there was an abundance of royal wine, reflecting the king's generosity. By edict of the king, no limits were placed on the drinking, for the king had instructed all his palace officials to serve each man as much as he wanted. At the same time, Queen Vashti gave a banquet for the women in the royal palace of King Xerxes."*

We have seen that king Xerxes organised a festival for 180 days in order to boast about his wealth and power. We have also seen that the last seven days of the festival were devoted to a banquet for everybody living in Susa.

We now read that the lavish meal included unlimited wine served in gold goblets. (The Persians were famous for their elaborate and unique drinking vessels.) This was unusual generosity as usually there was a strict limit on the amount of wine allowed to be consumed. Normally, the wine had to be the same as the king drank and only consumed when he proposed a toast.

Perhaps there was a reason for the generosity. It was not unusual for the king to try to buy support through bribery. Perhaps, as the next season for going to war approached, the king needed to expand his army and his recruiting officers were present at the feast. History records that Xerxes staged disastrous campaigns against Greece at this time.

Another reason the king allowed freedom to consume the wine as he did was because there were no women at the feast. And without women to bring their gentle character, the nature of the feast would be very different.

As the writer continues to set the scene, we are introduced to Queen Vashti. In another departure from the norm, the women held their own banquet. It was usual for both men and women to feast together. But we are not told the reason for this departure from normal etiquette.

The name "Vashti" means "the best, desired, beloved". It is probably a title for the favourite wife rather than her actual name. Other historians call her Amestris, the mother of Artaxerxes I who was king after Xerxes between 465-424 BC. The fact that her son became the next king after Xerxes is evidence that she returned to favour after the time of Esther.

We read that Vashti was beautiful. As the story progresses we find that Xerxes sought a replacement for Vashti with a beauty contest. Therefore, she was probably found by the same method. Vashti was the king's wife because of her outward beauty not because she had the best character for the position.

Queen Vashti is introduced when she is giving a feast to the women of Susa. Feasting is a prominent theme in Esther with banquets providing the setting for the important developments in the story. There are ten banquets in total. But it is the three pairs of banquets at the beginning, middle and end of the story which are particularly important.

The festivals of Israel also contain considerable opportunities for feasting but their purpose is very different. Xerxes used the feasts to promote himself. Israel's feasts are to promote the Lord and to celebrate what He has already achieved as well as what He will achieve in days to come.

King Xerxes and Queen Vashti held their feasts for a different reason. Their intention was to glorify themselves. They wanted their wealth and power to be feared throughout the Empire, especially hoping to intimidate the Greeks.

Today, we are also encouraged to feast. There is a time for fasting but we should not forget the feasting. What we read of the early followers of Jesus in the New Testament suggests that they fellowshipped each day around the meal table. And it is likely that each meal included wine. The purpose in fellowship was to feast on Jesus, encouraging each other with the words and gifts of Spirit (Acts 2:46-47).

Today, it is good to restore the practice of eating together in order to feast on the words and gifts of Jesus. A small step in the right direction is to have family meal times. Many families have forgotten how to eat together, each meal being taken in front of a TV or in haste in order to meet the next appointment.

A further move towards restoring our fellowship with God and each other is to have meals with our friends with the intention of listening to God as we eat. Jesus spoke some of His most remembered words at a meal table during His "Last Supper". In fact, much of the latter chapters in John's Gospel are an account of the words around a meal table.

Three

Esther 1:10-12 *"On the seventh day of the feast, when King Xerxes was in high spirits because of the wine, he told the seven eunuchs who attended him—Mehuman, Biztha, Harbona, Bigtha, Abagtha, Zethar, and Carcas— to bring Queen Vashti to him with the royal crown on her head. He wanted the nobles and all the other men to gaze on her beauty, for she was a very beautiful woman. But when they conveyed the king's order to Queen Vashti, she refused to come. This made the king furious, and he burned with anger."*

It was on the last day of the 180 days festival that the queen refused to obey the king, a decision which had devastating consequences for her and, eventually, for the many Jews living in the Empire.

It is no surprise that after six months feasting, with much wine, that the king was drunk. Having spent those months glorying in his wealth and power, Xerxes wanted finally to boast about his wife, possibly the most beautiful woman in the city.

King Xerxes had seven eunuchs to attend him. A servant was often castrated when his duties involved considerable contact with women, particularly with the king's harem. Perhaps the castration was a blessing to some because if he had fallen to temptation and molested one of the king's wives or concubines, the consequence would have been certain death.

The seven eunuchs who served the king did not only act as intermediaries with the harem. They had a variety of duties, often commanding a great deal of power.

The names of the eunuchs might be nicknames given to recognise their individual characteristics. It is helpful to realise their origin, some, such as Mehuman, being distinctly Hebrew. We often read names without realising their origin. But as we uncover more about them we realise that God has many of His servants in places of influence.

Mehuman means "One who is faithful". It is a name which could have been given at birth to encourage a child to become a faithful person. But it is more likely to be a name to recognise the character which had grown over many years. A king would want a faithful person for his servant.

The web contains several different definitions for Biztha but the most common is "bound". It probably represents the fact that Biztha was a eunuch, bound to serve the king.

Harbona means "ass-driver", possibly given in recognition of his character. A person who bosses others is often called something like that.

Bigtha means "a garden", or "gift of fortune". Abagtha, means "fortunate one". Zethar means "He that examines or beholds" and Carcas means "the covering of a lamb".

These eunuchs were given the task to bring Queen Vashti to King Xerxes so that he could proudly show her to the men in his kingdom as if she were a prized possession. We are not told why this task required seven men but it seems that each was involved. It is likely that the queen would have to be carried into the banqueting hall in her royal clothes wearing the crown and it might have been the responsibility of the eunuchs to give her the prominence expected.

The Queen refused the king's request. We are not told the reason for her unwise refusal although history records that it was unusual for the king to expect his wife to be paraded in front of male guests in the way Xerxes required. It is also possible that the queen and king had argued during the season of feasting to the extent that Vashti wanted to retaliate for the drunken behaviour of the king.

We do not know the reason for the refusal but we do know that the queen was expected to obey the king, whose word could not be opposed. Knowing that Xerxes was a violent man, it is not surprising that he was angry with Vashti. What is surprising is that Vashti thought she could disobey him.

Today, many men still expect instant obedience from their wives. Strangely, it is an expectation demanded more frequently from men with a religious background. But, it is not the relationship taught by Jesus and the early disciples. And it is not the response we should demand from our wives today.

A marriage is a partnership of equals. When we marry we leave our individual status and become one new entity. Together, we are called to serve God and each other. It is true that we are different, with individual gifts and abilities. But it is as we both contribute the gifts which God has invested in us individually that we are able to serve Him together (1 Peter 3:7).

A husband needs to submit to his wife just as much as the wife submits to her husband. When Paul wrote to the Christians in Ephesus, he advised that they should submit to each other (Ephesians 5:21) He followed that general advice with a more specific warning to the wives at Ephesus reinforcing that they should submit to their husbands. The reason for his emphasis was that the Ephesian wives were used to ruling their husbands because the goddess in that city was Diana. And the worship of Diana was governed by women. Paul reinforced that the Ephesian wives should no longer rule their husbands but submit to them just as the husbands were also submitting.

We submit, not to the person but to the Spirit of God within each one. The purpose of submission is to come to an agreement with the will of God. Therefore, we discuss what each feels is God's heart until we come to an agreement in faith.

A husband who expects obedience from his wife regardless of whether he knows the will of God takes the position of a god. It is a dangerous position to take.

Four

Esther 1:13-15 *"He immediately consulted with his wise advisers, who knew all the Persian laws and customs, for he always asked their advice. The names of these men were Carshena, Shethar, Admatha, Tarshish, Meres, Marsena, and Memucan—seven nobles of Persia and Media. They met with the king regularly and held the highest positions in the empire. "What must be done to Queen Vashti?" the king demanded. "What penalty does the law provide for a queen who refuses to obey the king's orders, properly sent through his eunuchs?" "*

The king did not know how to respond to his wife's open display of rebellion. He might have been able to forgive her disobedience to him if it had been committed in private but it had been done in such a way that all the men of the city knew of her rebellion. If it had been a private matter the king need not have consulted his counsellors. But, in view of the public disgrace he felt, he had to deal with it publicly.

The seven wise advisers, men who knew the laws and customs of Persia, were asked to advise the king what he should do. Today, we would probably advise mediation to bring the king and queen together and rebuild their broken relationship. But the advisers were not asked to heal the relationship. The king wanted to know what punishment he could deliver.

Unlike the earlier eunuchs, the names of the wise men were probably those given at birth because the meanings do not seem to associate with nicknames. Many of the names have a Hebrew origin but this could be because they have been translated into that language for a Jewish readership.

Alternatively, it could be indicative of the esteem the king gave to the wisdom in Israel, although we will find that Xerxes did not seem to have any knowledge of the specific nationalities of the people who served him.

Carshena means "a lamb, sleeping". Shethar means "putrefied, searching" or "seeking to rot". Admatha can be a name for a man or a woman and has a variety of meanings such as "unconquered", "a cloud of death", "a mortal vapour" and some suggestions linked to moon signs. Tashish, again has a variety of meanings such as "the sea coast", "to break down or shatter", "chrysolite" or "precious stone". Meres means "defluxion; imposthume". A defluxion is a copious discharge of fluid matter, an inflammation or a sudden loss of hair. An imposthume is an abscess. Neither definition for Meres seems complimentary. Marsena means "bitterness of a bramble "or "worthy". Lastly, Memucan means " impoverished", "to prepare", "certain", or "true".

Memucan, although mentioned last, was the senior adviser with the most prominent position in the land behind the king.

In his anger, king Xerxes demanded to know what could be done with his queen. In his opinion he had followed the correct protocol by sending his eunuchs to bring queen Vashti to him. He could not understand why she would have decided to disobey his order. We are not told whether he sought to find out if his wife had a good reason for her refusal. All that we know is that he immediately sought revenge.

Today, we often face a similar challenge to that faced by king Xerxes. The details will be different as it will not necessarily be our spouse who defies us. But, our will can be challenged when we do not obtain what we want. How we respond to the challenge defines our spiritual maturity.

Our will is what course of action we decide to take throughout each day. Every decision we make is a choice about what we will allow to happen. And when our will only allows what we want for ourselves, we frequently become frustrated because what we want does not happen. King Xerxes was used to people giving him what he wanted. He did not know how to deal with a situation when his will was being ignored. It is the same for many today.

If we are born of God, our challenge is to live by the will of God instead of our own will. It is a challenge which we need to accept before we are born of the Spirit so that we receive the mind of Christ at our new birth. Sadly, over the last century, the challenge to exchange our will for the will of God has been lost because we have watered down the new birth experience. The message people are given today is one of receiving something from God instead of an exchange of wills. The truth is that we can only receive from God when we give ourselves to Him. We exchange our will for His will.

When we exchange our will, we no longer demand what we want. We only want what God wants. Consequently, we no longer become frustrated when we do not receive what we demand. We are able to concentrate on building relationships; able to concentrate on forgiveness and reconciliation instead of revenge.

Five

Esther 1:16-22 *"Memucan answered the king and his nobles, "Queen Vashti has wronged not only the king but also every noble and citizen throughout your empire. Women everywhere will begin to despise their husbands when they learn that Queen Vashti has refused to appear before the king. Before this day is out, the wives of all the king's nobles throughout Persia and Media will hear what the queen did and will start treating their husbands the same way. There will be no end to their contempt and anger. "So if it please the king, we suggest that you issue a written decree, a law of the Persians and Medes that cannot be revoked. It should order that Queen Vashti be forever banished from the presence of King Xerxes, and that the king should choose another queen more worthy than she. When this decree is published throughout the king's vast empire, husbands everywhere, whatever their rank, will receive proper respect from their wives!" The king and his nobles thought this made good sense, so he followed Memucan's counsel. He sent letters to all parts of the empire, to each province in its own script and language, proclaiming that every man should be the ruler of his own home and should say whatever he pleases."*

The king asked his wise men for legal advice. He wanted to know if Queen Vashti had violated a law which would determine her punishment. But he did not receive any legal advice. Instead, his wise men responded out of fear that the cultural and social structure could be undermined. They were determined that male power would continue.

Memucan spoke for all the wise men when he answered the king's request for advice. And because Queen Vashti's behaviour had already become a major incident he addressed the king with all his nobles present. His comments reveal the influence that the queen held in the Empire.

Memucan's advice to the king demonstrates that wives throughout the empire were expected to obey their husbands without question or delay. It is possible that the queen deliberately rebelled in order to make a political point about the liberation of women. If that was Vashti's intention, her plan badly misfired. Instead of gaining better treatment for wives throughout the empire, she gave an excuse for men to have greater power over their spouse.

In reality, the edict sent to give husbands their greater rights would not have made much difference to the way wives were treated. Men would continue in the way they always had. If a husband loved his wife, he would continue to love her and give freedom to choose how she lived. If a husband saw his wife as his slave, he would continue to do so.

Today, there are laws in many countries giving rights to wives. But the law does not change an individual's attitude. A law might force a different behaviour but what a person thinks will rarely change. And when a challenge arises the law is forgotten as the attitude takes over.

We change our attitude when we have revelation of something better. Today, we have the advantage over the Medes and Persians because we have the Spirit of God working in our lives to bring revelation. The truth is that we do not begin life as perfect individuals. But we have a promise from God that He will transform us into the image of Christ as we renew our minds (Romans 12:2).

Queen Vashti was deposed by the edict written by the king banishing her from the king's presence forever. And we are told that the law of the Medes and Persians could not be revoked. Therefore, the consequence of the queen's act of rebellion to not go into the king's presence was that she was banished from that presence forever. What she wanted temporarily became permanent.

History records that Queen Vashti's banishment was not permanent as she bore several more children with King Xerxes after this record of Queen Esther. But we are not told how the irreversible law was finally reversed.

The king sent letters throughout the empire giving husbands the right to say what they wanted in their houses in their own language. It might seem a strange right today but there was much intermarriage between different races and cultures in the time of Xerxes. The wives would speak their own tongue which was often unintelligible to the household. The king's edict made it compulsory that the language of the husband became spoken instead.

The challenge that Queen Vashti gave to the king was "who reigns?" or "who is in control?". Today, the world faces the same challenge. Every nation is ruled by someone who wants to be in control. And every marriage has the same challenge to answer. It is the same for an individual. Who is in control of our lives?

The answer is simple. We give control to whomever or whatever we allow to rule over us. We can do that voluntarily or under compulsion. However, God does not want us to be controlled by anyone or anything. He created us to live in freedom; to live in freedom to choose to respond to Him.

The truth is that we can live in spiritual freedom even when we are controlled by a person. We live in freedom by learning how to hear and obey the Spirit of God. When we can do that, we are in perfect freedom regardless of our situation. We are able to serve God as we serve a person. As we serve God, we find that serving a person in humility and love can be God's way of transforming our character.

Six

Esther 2:1-4 *"But after Xerxes' anger had subsided, he began thinking about Vashti and what she had done and the decree he had made. So his personal attendants suggested, "Let us search the empire to find beautiful young virgins for the king. Let the king appoint agents in each province to bring these beautiful young women into the royal harem at the fortress of Susa. Hegai, the king's eunuch in charge of the harem, will see that they are all given beauty treatments. After that, the young woman who most pleases the king will be made queen instead of Vashti." This advice was very appealing to the king, so he put the plan into effect."*

Having deposed Vashti, Xerxes waged an unsuccessful war against Greece over the following four years. Although we are not told when the plan to find a replacement for Vashti was followed, it was probably executed when the king was at war as it required a search for suitable candidates throughout the Empire, which would take considerable time.

We are told that king Xerxes began to think about Vashti after his anger had subsided. He began to wonder whether he had overreacted in the heat of the moment. The truth is that we rarely make good decisions when we are angry. It is usually best to wait until our anger has cooled before making any important choices.

On the surface, we are told the king's thoughts were about Vashti's actions and his edicts, but he was really thinking about his needs. He was probably regretting his decision to banish his wife and wanted to know if it could be repealed. But when he informed the advisers about his needs they concocted a new plan which did not include bringing Vashti and the king together again. Instead they suggested a beauty contest drawing virgins from every part of the empire to Susa.

This was an enormous undertaking as the virgins would be accompanied with others to provide for her. We are not told how many beautiful virgins were found but as we read the story we find there were many.

The Hebrew name for the eunuch in charge of the harem was Hegai, which has many suggested meanings such as: "Meditation, word, groaning, separation, suitable, fit, worthy". He was responsible for preparing each virgin to make her acceptable for the king with beauty treatments which could have been applied for as long as a year.

Today, as we read Esther's story, we might consider that it is not suitable for someone to enter a beauty contest in order to find a husband. But Esther had no choice. If she had refused to comply with the king's edict, she would have been killed. In that respect, there are many similarities with the stories of Esther and Joseph. Joseph was a slave, forced to do what his master ordered. Even so, he became the most powerful man in Egypt other than Pharaoh.

Both Esther and Joseph overcame their challenges by using the gifts God gave them. Esther had a gift of beauty whilst Joseph could understand dreams. As well as those gifts, they were full of integrity and humility, willing to submit to God in whatever challenges they had to face.

We also have gifts given by God to enable us to fulfil our purpose. And when we face challenges, we often find that we can overcome them by using the gift which God has given. The gift is a key to opening doors when we know how to use it.

There is a great variety of gifts given by God. Some are obvious whilst others seem less so. Sadly, we tend to minimise the gifts God has given us whilst we look at the gifts of others with envy. In doing this we dishonour God, effectively telling Him He does not know what He is doing.

Some examples of this are as follows. Many beautiful women treat their beauty as a curse. People who dream often prefer to have dreamless nights. Those with a gift of serving prefer to be served. A gift of giving is often hindered by a miserly spirit.

We should never despise the gifts God gives. Instead we should seek to find them and use them in faith.

Seven

Esther 2:5-9 *"At that time there was a Jewish man in the fortress of Susa whose name was Mordecai son of Jair. He was from the tribe of Benjamin and was a descendant of Kish and Shimei. His family had been among those who, with King Jehoiachin of Judah, had been exiled from Jerusalem to Babylon by King Nebuchadnezzar. This man had a very beautiful and lovely young cousin, Hadassah, who was also called Esther. When her father and mother died, Mordecai adopted her into his family and raised her as his own daughter. As a result of the king's decree, Esther, along with many other young women, was brought to the king's harem at the fortress of Susa and placed in Hegai's care. Hegai was very impressed with Esther and treated her kindly. He quickly ordered a special menu for her and provided her with beauty treatments. He also assigned her seven maids specially chosen from the king's palace, and he moved her and her maids into the best place in the harem."*

Despite him being a Jew, we are not told the Hebrew name for Mordecai. Instead we know his Persian name which was probably derived from that of the Babylonian god Marduk. Some historians associate Mordecai with a senior advisor to the King with that name who was responsible for the accounts, although that is not certain.

Mordecai was a Benjaminite, a tribe recognised for its fighting prowess. His ancestors included Kish and Shimei who were either the names of those taken into exile 100 years earlier with King Jehoiachin or the more famous heroes of previous centuries. Kish was the father of King Saul (1 Samuel 9:1).

Shimei threw stones at David when he fled from Absalom (2 Samuel 16:5).

In the exile to Babylon, the Jews had been dispersed throughout the Empire some, such as Mordecai's family, to Susa. Wherever they lived, many Jews rose to positions of prominence. And people like Daniel and Esther became the most influential people in the Empire.

The truth is that God always cares for us. Whatever situation we find ourselves in, God is already working out a solution for our problem. He saw the problem coming and put a rescue plan into operation for when it was needed. But as with Esther and Joseph, what seemed like a challenge in their life, was necessary for God to fulfil His eternal purposes.

Esther was either the cousin or niece of Mordecai. The culture and language does not make an exact translation of the original words possible. It is similar in many cultures today. In Kenya, for example, we are often confused by what we are told concerning relationships because the language does not allow for clear descriptions.

Hadassah is Esther's Hebrew name, meaning "myrtle." The name Esther could either come from the Persian word for "star," or from the name of the Babylonian goddess Ishtar.

Esther, gifted with beauty, was taken with the other contestants to the king's harem under the care of Hegai. She had no choice. We need to realise that when we have no choice in the situations we face, God is with us. He has a plan for our salvation. Things might look desperate. But He is able to deliver us. In the event He wants us to go through a difficult challenge, He is still with us to give us strength, perseverance, and hope.

As David said "Even when I walk through the darkest valley, I will not be afraid, for you are close beside me. Your rod and your staff protect and comfort me (Psalms 23:4).

Esther found favour with Hegai. We are not told why she found favour but we can imagine it was not because of her beauty. There were many beautiful women in the harem. But Esther stood out because she was different in her spirit. And Hegai gave her and her seven maids the best living quarters.

Esther had to become ready to meet the king. She had special ointments and food to ensure she was suitable to please Xerxes when her time for appraisal arrived.

This is a simple description of the time we live in today. Xerxes, despite not being a Jew and being a tyrant, is a symbol of King Jesus. We are waiting for a day in which we will stand before God, the Judge, to know whether we are allowed to be part of the great marriage feast. It is the time for us to make ourselves ready.

There are seven maids to help us prepare. Seven is the number for completion or perfection. The maids are symbolic of Holy Spirit, who is our helper (John 16). Our food is the word of God, Jesus. The special ointments are the work of the Spirit of God within us who transforms us into the image of Christ.

There are many other maidens competing for the honour to be married to the king. This speaks of the different religions and philosophies which give opposing roads to utopia. But, there is only one position available for the bride. For us to be part of her, we have to be able to "eat and smell" of Jesus.

Eight

Esther 2:10-15 *"Esther had not told anyone of her nationality and family background, because Mordecai had directed her not to do so. Every day Mordecai would take a walk near the courtyard of the harem to find out about Esther and what was happening to her. Before each young woman was taken to the king's bed, she was given the prescribed twelve months of beauty treatments—six months with oil of myrrh, followed by six months with special perfumes and ointments. When it was time for her to go to the king's palace, she was given her choice of whatever clothing or jewellery she wanted to take from the harem. That evening she was taken to the king's private rooms, and the next morning she was brought to the second harem, where the king's wives lived. There she would be under the care of Shaashgaz, the king's eunuch in charge of the concubines. She would never go to the king again unless he had especially enjoyed her and requested her by name."*

On the advice of Mordecai, Esther did not speak about her nationality or family to anyone. We are not told why Mordecai gave this advice but it is possible that he realised the discrimination Esther would receive if her Jewish background was known. As the story unfolds, we realise the old hostility between the Amalekites and Israel is at the centre and king Xerxes had appointed some Amalekites to important positions of influence.

Today, we encourage each other to share our faith believing it is our duty to do so. Sometimes this is good, but not always. We need to be sensitive to what God asks of us in each situation.

Often we speak too quickly and in our haste we raise a stumbling block to the people we speak to. It is better to build a relationship bridge of trust and honesty before trying to persuade anyone to believe what we say.

Mordecai continued to care for his younger cousin taking time each day to enquire about her welfare in the harem. Although it was no longer his responsibility to provide for Esther, Mordecai did not forget his cousin. Today, we do not always take such care over our relationships. Instead, when circumstances force people out of direct contact we can quickly forget them. However, we need to sensitive to what God is asking from us. He might well want us to care for people despite not being "responsible" for them.

Each virgin was given 12 months to prepare for a one night "interview" with the king. That one night would determine whether she would become the next queen or spend the rest of her life in the second harem as a concubine of the king, always available should he wish to spend time with her. In essence it was the life of a widow living in relative opulence.

Although we are only told about the beauty treatment the virgins received, the time of preparation would include training about court etiquette, language and social skills. The 12 months preparation was divided into two periods of 6 months for the purpose of developing external beauty. During the first period, oil of myrrh was used, a traditional spice used as a beauty treatment. It has traditionally been understood to symbolise death but today is seen as prophesying life and blessing. In reality we can accept both meanings because it is only as we die to our old nature that we receive the new life and blessings that God gives.

Esther entered the first harem as an equal with many other virgins. She was given the same beauty treatment; given the same education as the others. She had no understanding how the king could determine which virgin would become the next queen. The king would make his decision based on criteria only he knew. She had no alternative but to seek the Lord and trust Him for her future.

Today, we are often in a situation where we are at the mercy of others. Our lives depend on the whims and choices of people we do not know. Perhaps we compete with others for a job which we desperately want. But we cannot obtain it unless someone else decides to offer it. Perhaps we need a loan from the bank or someone else with money to share. But we are not alone and have to compete with others for the opportunity to receive the money we need.

Have we learned to trust the Lord in every situation? Do we believe the Lord knows our needs and loves us enough to supply them? Do we have the faith to trust Him? Or do we become frustrated by our failure to obtain what we want?

The truth is we need to be "anointed with myrrh" for a period of time. We have to die to our old nature. We have to die to things we want. And in death, we will find the Lord gives His life. He takes us on a journey with Him; a journey which opens new doors and new opportunities. It is a journey full of life and blessings.

Nine

Esther 2:15-18 *"Esther was the daughter of Abihail, who was Mordecai's uncle. (Mordecai had adopted his younger cousin Esther.) When it was Esther's turn to go to the king, she accepted the advice of Hegai, the eunuch in charge of the harem. She asked for nothing except what he suggested, and she was admired by everyone who saw her. Esther was taken to King Xerxes at the royal palace in early winter of the seventh year of his reign. And the king loved Esther more than any of the other young women. He was so delighted with her that he set the royal crown on her head and declared her queen instead of Vashti. To celebrate the occasion, he gave a great banquet in Esther's honour for all his nobles and officials, declaring a public holiday for the provinces and giving generous gifts to everyone."*

Esther did not enter the harem of the king resigned to being a widow for the rest of her life. She attempted to win the king's favour in order to become the queen. She was not content with being second best or an also ran.

What is our attitude in the challenges we face? Do we expect to win? Or have we become so used to failure that we no longer expect to succeed? The truth is that when we enter a battle which concerns the kingdom of God we can expect to win. God often allows us to lose other battles which concern our old, earthly, nature because we have to learn to walk in the Spirit, not in our flesh.

Esther had a submissive spirit and accepted the advice of Hegai. That advice dealt with her clothes and food, her speech and deportment. Esther submitted to anything that Hegai taught her because she knew that he favoured her above the other women. She could trust his advice because she knew he wanted her to succeed.

Today, we also need to develop a submissive spirit. We submit to everything the Spirit of God asks of us. Sometimes God speaks to us through other people and we need to learn to submit to Him when we hear His voice through others. But we need to be wise when we listen to others because they do not always speak the words of God or in the Spirit of God. The truth is that we are responsible for our actions and our decisions. We will not be able to blame someone else for what we have done when we stand before God on the Day of Judgement.

Esther was taken to the King in the winter during the seventh year of his reign. She had prepared for this moment for a full year. She was ready. We do not know whether she expected to be chosen as the next queen but she was prepared in case she was chosen. The result was that the king was captivated by her beauty and her character.

Are people captivated by us? We might not have handsome external features as Esther. We cannot change the body which God has given us. But, our features can change through our laughter and our peace. A miserable person brings darkness wherever they visit. And their misery causes their features to look brooding. A joyful person brings laughter. A peaceful person brings their peace to settle any disturbance.

When we enter a spiritual battle we need the joy of the Lord to give us strength. We need His peace, His faith and His love. It is the character of God which overcomes our enemy. And Esther entered the king's presence with God's character and captivated him.

King Xerxes needed one night only to decide that Esther was to be his queen. He placed the crown upon her head and honoured her with a great banquet. This is a picture of our relationship with Jesus. Many people are rejected by Him because they do not have a desire for His Spirit. But there is only one way for us to be accepted by God. We come to Him in submission, acknowledging that Jesus gave His life as a sacrifice for our sin. There is no other way. Esther came to the king in submission acknowledging that her future as queen depended on him alone.

Previously when the king held a banquet, he dishonoured his wife, Vashti. But now, the king honoured Esther as he introduced her to his nobles and subjects. Such was his pleasure in his new wife that Xerxes declared a public holiday, which probably included such things as the remission of taxes and the release of slaves.

Today, we live at a time when the Church is not yet honoured in the world. Individually, we are accepted by God when we have faith in the sacrifice of Jesus for us. But our divisions and worldliness do not set us apart as different to anyone else. However, a time is coming when we will be honoured in the world and many will flock to become part of the Body of Christ.

At the time of Esther, the temple had been rebuilt in Jerusalem by the remnant Jews. This is a picture of the committed Christians today who are seeking the Kingdom of God above everything else. As the power and authority of God is revealed in that remnant, the Church will begin to live in harmony and there will be a harvest of souls. At that time the Church will be honoured by the world.

Ten

Esther 2:19-23 *"Even after all the young women had been transferred to the second harem and Mordecai had become a palace official, Esther continued to keep her family background and nationality a secret. She was still following Mordecai's directions, just as she did when she lived in his home. One day as Mordecai was on duty at the king's gate, two of the king's eunuchs, Bigthana and Teresh—who were guards at the door of the king's private quarters—became angry at King Xerxes and plotted to assassinate him. But Mordecai heard about the plot and gave the information to Queen Esther. She then told the king about it and gave Mordecai credit for the report. When an investigation was made and Mordecai's story was found to be true, the two men were impaled on a sharpened pole. This was all recorded in The Book of the History of King Xerxes' Reign."*

Many virgins had been taken from their homes to become concubines of the king, each one hoping to become the next queen. Their lives, and the lives of their families, were disturbed at the whim of the king. Yet many never had the opportunity to spend the night with the king. Many had no opportunity to impress him because the king chose Esther in the middle of the "beauty contest". The fate of all the virgins chosen for the king was to spend the remaining days of their lives in the harem as concubines. It is true that they were given every comfort they needed, far more than they could expect in their homes but their lives lacked any real purpose, unless they determined to do more than they were required.

Many today suffer similar consequences from the actions of others. Events can occur which suddenly turn our lives upside down and we find we have no purpose. Perhaps our spouse dies. Perhaps we have an accident which leaves a disability or we lose a high-powered job through no fault of our own. Suddenly our lives lose their purpose. How do we respond?

In reality, there is only one sensible way to respond to life changing events. We need God's perspective each time. As soon as we hear Him speak, we find peace and hope for a purposeful future rises again.

Esther continued to keep her nationality secret from the king and the court even though Mordecai was promoted to an important position as a palace official. She continued to submit to her wise cousin even though she was in a far more prominent position than he. Today, we are sensible to submit in the same way to those who are wise. Our position counts for nothing before God. All that is important is what He says through His people.

Mordecai was given a position at the king's gate, the place in the city where important decisions were made. There was usually a market at the gate to the city and the king gave court decisions from there as it was both the commercial and social centre. History records a Mordecai being the court treasurer at this time. If that was the same person, it would be sensible for him to work from the city gate where the commercial activity took place.

Mordecai overheard a plot to assassinate the king whilst he worked. This is one of the many "coincidences" which demonstrates the faithfulness of God to us. But it also demonstrates the importance of our acting on what we hear. Mordecai could have ignored what he heard and allowed others to do what they wanted. Instead, he acted informing Esther that there was a plot to kill her husband. Esther told the king, giving credit to Mordecai. We will find that if Esther had not told the king, there would have been a different ending to the story.

The king investigated to establish the truth of Mordecai's report and found there was indeed a plot against him. And having found the truth, he ordered the execution of the two men involved. A report of the plot and investigation was written in the court annals.

This event shows the importance of dealing with gossip wisely. Some people have a policy to never act on gossip, believing that gossip is always bad. And it is true that Jesus tells us not to gossip. The truth is that we should never repeat what we hear in order to idly talk about people and situations. That is wrong and we need to discourage that sort of behaviour. But, we need to encourage sharing life so we can pray together about and for the people who face the challenges we discuss.

Mordecai did not idly repeat the gossip he heard. He wanted to save the life of the king. And when the king heard he did not act on the gossip without question. He first investigated to establish whether it was true. But, when knowing the truth, he dealt with it accordingly.

We always need to ensure we act on the truth. Today, there is much deception. Our enemy is the father of lies and has a web of deception throughout the world. Fake news is everywhere. And we can waste much time worrying about something that will never happen.

When we hear gossip, we need to first go to God and ask Him what we should do about it. He might give a word of knowledge which leads to a solution. In any event, He will want us to establish the truth before we act.

We do not always know the importance of the things we hear. Sometimes, a chance remark will be life-changing. It is only by living close with the Spirit of God that we can find His wisdom and direction.

Eleven

Esther 3:1-4 *"Some time later King Xerxes promoted Haman son of Hammedatha the Agagite over all the other nobles, making him the most powerful official in the empire. All the king's officials would bow down before Haman to show him respect whenever he passed by, for so the king had commanded. But Mordecai refused to bow down or show him respect. Then the palace officials at the king's gate asked Mordecai, "Why are you disobeying the king's command?" They spoke to him day after day, but still he refused to comply with the order. So they spoke to Haman about this to see if he would tolerate Mordecai's conduct, since Mordecai had told them he was a Jew."*

It was four years after Mordecai exposed the plot to assassinate the king that Xerxes promoted Haman to the most prominent position in the empire. Haman was descended from Agag, the Amalekite king eventually killed by Samuel after Saul's initial disobedience (1 Samuel 15).

There was intense hatred between Israel and the Amalekites, an animosity which started during Israel's time in the wilderness before they entered the Promised Land. The Amalekites had attacked Israel and the Lord declared He would be at war with them for all generations, and He asked Israel to "blot out the name of Amalek from under heaven" (Ex 17:8-16; Dt 25:19).

King Saul's obedience to God was tested when the Lord asked him to fulfil the requirement to blot out the name of Amalek. Although Saul attacked the tribe, killing many, he initially decided to keep King Agag and the cattle alive (1Sa 15). Samuel later killed Agag but many believe that the wife of Agag escaped with her children to enable the tribe to continue. Now, centuries after that battle led by the Benjamite King Saul, the Benjamite Mordecai continues the war with the Amalekites.

No reason is given for the promotion of Haman to his powerful position. Ironically, Mordecai had not been rewarded for saving the king, an act which deserved some recognition. But Haman is given recognition, apparently for doing nothing. Today, we see similar injustice everywhere. And it is probable that we experience it at some time in our lives when we are overlooked for the benefit of someone with less experience and ability.

In such a situation we are tempted to be jealous and to become frustrated. It is better to follow the example of Mordecai who did not allow temptation to overcome him. Instead, he trusted the Lord.

Haman, a proud man, expected the king's officials, including Mordecai, to bow down to him. He was, in fact, in a senior position to Mordecai and the custom was that juniors bowed down to seniors. There was no inherent reason why Mordecai did not bow before Haman. There was no commandment forbidding Jews to bow before others to show their respect. The only reason for Mordecai's action was that Haman was an Amalekite.

When the palace officials asked Mordecai the reason for his disrespect he told them he was a Jew, revealing the long history of hostility. And, the palace officials asked Haman whether he would tolerate Mordecai's conduct.

We see the character of Mordecai in his actions. I wonder if we have the same character. He was determined to serve the Lord with integrity, obeying ancient commands with no apparent relevance to his personal situation. Today, we are often faced with a similar dilemma. We live in a world which does not always follow the old commands of the Lord. Our attitude towards marriage, sexuality, honesty, integrity and many other aspects of life is challenged each day. Are we prepared to be bold by obeying the heart of the Lord?

Today, we are often afraid to stand out because we are different. We have peer pressure and the desire to be part of a friendship group. Each group develops unspoken social codes. Each group has its membership rules. And we are not welcome when we stand against the group standards. It is still similar in many churches where anyone who disagrees with doctrine or there is a personality clash is advised to leave.

The specific issue that Mordecai challenged was submission. He was not prepared to submit to a person who was an enemy of the Lord. Queen Vashti's refusal to submit to Xerxes was the issue which destroyed their relationship. Esther, on the other hand, was prepared to submit to Mordecai and Hegai. Today, submission continues to be a challenge which we have to overcome. Are we prepared to stand against ungodly people? We cannot make such a stand without knowing the heart of the Lord. And it requires boldness and simple trust that the Lord will use our stand to bring about His purposes.

Twelve

Esther 3:5-7 *"When Haman saw that Mordecai would not bow down or show him respect, he was filled with rage. He had learned of Mordecai's nationality, so he decided it was not enough to lay hands on Mordecai alone. Instead, he looked for a way to destroy all the Jews throughout the entire empire of Xerxes. So in the month of April, during the twelfth year of King Xerxes' reign, lots were cast in Haman's presence (the lots were called Purim) to determine the best day and month to take action. And the day selected was March 7, nearly a year later."*

Haman, the Amalekite and sworn enemy of Israel, was filled with rage when he realised that Mordecai, a Jew, would not bow to him. Essentially, his pride was piqued and he responded in the same way that king Xerxes had when his pride was also offended by Vashti. He wanted to destroy the person who had offended. But it is there that the similarity ends. Xerxes regretted his actions and wanted to repeal his decision. But Haman's rage increased to the extent he wanted to destroy all Jews throughout the empire.

Today, our pride continues to be the source of much conflict. Pride makes us want to be the central figure and the most important person. And when pride is added to our prejudices against an individual or group, we want to destroy everyone who stands against what we want.

But there was another dimension to the hatred which Haman felt towards Israel. Satan saw an opportunity to destroy God's chosen people. And he knew that if he could destroy all Israel, the promised Messiah could not be born. Satan always seeks to destroy anyone who has the potential to be the Saviour of the world.

Today we are beginning to see the church coming together in harmony. And when we find that true harmony there will be a worldwide harvest as men and women take their place in the Kingdom of God. That will be a season when the world will see the love, the power and the authority of God in His people in a way it has never been seen before. Satan also knows that this season fast approaches. And he will seek to destroy the people of God before that harvest can be brought in.

It is the two issues of pride and submission which will contribute to the coming conflict. When God's people decide that they cannot bow to the demands of the world any longer, the world will turn against them. It is then that the church will turn to God in humility and love and experience His deliverance.

Haman waited until the fourteenth year of Xerxes reign before he acted on his hatred. Esther was in her fifth year as queen. They had been years of peace for Jews, with no warning that danger was approaching.

Haman cast lots to determine the best time to take action against the Jews. The lots were called "Purim" in the original language from which the Jewish Festival of Purim, which remembers the events of Esther, takes its name.

The principle of casting lots is the same as throwing dice or reading cards. Those participating had faith that the lots would forecast what they wanted to know. It was a common practice, even used by Jews on occasions. In fact, the replacement for Judas Iscariot by the early Church was found by casting lots (Acts 1:21-26). Although it is not a recommended means to find the will of God, it is possible He will respond to our faith if we totally trust Him to show His will through casting lots.

Haman asked the soothsayers to throw the lots in April, nearly a year before the date on which he was advised to take his action. If he had been a reasonable man, Haman's rage would have subsided during that time. But Haman was driven by hatred; a hatred fuelled by Satan's desire to destroy God's people.

There have been many similar seasons in history when Satan has sought to destroy Israel, such as through Hitler during the Second World War. But, when we understand that Christians have been born into true Israel (Romans 11:17), we realise that we also are destined to be under the threat of extinction. In fact, in many parts of the world, Christians face death every day.

Knowing this, we are wise to prepare for times of difficulty. It is good to practice with the spiritual weapons we have been given, such as fasting. For some, the idea of missing a meal seems impossible. But, if our future depends on that simple action, it is wise to explore how to act on it.

Thirteen

Esther 3:8-11 *"Then Haman approached King Xerxes and said, "There is a certain race of people scattered through all the provinces of your empire who keep themselves separate from everyone else. Their laws are different from those of any other people, and they refuse to obey the laws of the king. So it is not in the king's interest to let them live. If it pleases the king, issue a decree that they be destroyed, and I will give 10,000 large sacks of silver to the government administrators to be deposited in the royal treasury." The king agreed, confirming his decision by removing his signet ring from his finger and giving it to Haman son of Hammedatha the Agagite, the enemy of the Jews. The king said, "The money and the people are both yours to do with as you see fit.""*

Haman quickly followed the advice of the soothsayers and approached the king to spring the trap to exterminate the Jews. Haman's plan depended on the king's agreement, which he obtained by deception.

Haman withheld the name of the "certain race" when he described the rebellion of the Jews. If he had openly accused the Jews, the king would have realised the falseness of the deception because many of his trusted advisers and officials were from Israel. And he knew they were innocent of the charges.

It is true the Jews kept themselves separate. They tended to intermarry within tight communities and resisted integration although the fact that Esther had married the king proved the falseness of the deception.

It is also true that the laws of the Jews were different. They followed the Law of Moses which had specific dietary and religious requirements. But this was not rebellious because the laws of the Medes and Persians gave considerable freedom to all races within the empire to follow their own religions.

It was not true that the Jews refused to obey the laws of the king, although in one respect it was true in that Mordecai refused to bow to Haman. Ironically, the prophet Jeremiah had specifically advised the Jews in captivity in Babylon to do everything to bring peace where they lived: *"And work for the peace and prosperity of the city where I sent you into exile. Pray to the LORD for it, for its welfare will determine your welfare"* (Jeremiah 29:7).

When Haman told the king that it was not in the king's best interests to let the Jews live he played on the king's fears in the same way as Memucan had done when he suggested Vashti should be replaced (Esther 1:6).

Such was Haman's influence, the king accepted Haman's accusations without investigating their validity. This tells us much about the ruthlessness of Xerxes in that he could decide to destroy a whole race without even knowing who it was. It also reveals his insecurity in that he was obsessed with his safety.

Today, like Xerxes, until we have learned to be obedient to the Spirit of God, our decisions are still controlled by our emotions. And our emotions rarely give us a good foundation from which to make any decisions. We need to learn to hear and obey the Spirit of God in order to release His will and purposes on earth.

In a final attempt to obtain the king's agreement, Haman offered an enormous bribe of 10,000 talents, or 375 tons, of silver. Apparently, the annual income of the Persian Empire was 15,000 talents. Therefore, Haman bribed the king with two thirds of this amount. Haman probably expected to obtain such a vast sum through confiscating the wealth of the Jews he expected to slaughter.

The king's signet ring gave the seal of approval for all official policies. Any decision had to be signed with the seal and insignia of the king's ring. By giving his signet ring to Haman, the king signified that Haman had complete authority to seal the decree.

Although Haman had given several reasons to the king for the destruction of the Jews, it was probably the bribe which "sealed the deal". The king might have followed custom by seeming to give the money back to Haman but it is clear as the story unfolds that he would take possession of the bribe eventually.

Today, bribery continues to be a temptation which seals many decisions. It is a temptation we need to overcome in order to live righteously before God. But, in the coming battles against darkness, bribery will be a tool Satan uses in his attempt to destroy the people of God. Already, many nations are led by people willing to take a bribe. When the sums offered promise unbelievable wealth, few will be able to resist Satan's temptation.

Fourteen

Esther 3:12-15 *"So on April 17 the king's secretaries were summoned, and a decree was written exactly as Haman dictated. It was sent to the king's highest officers, the governors of the respective provinces, and the nobles of each province in their own scripts and languages. The decree was written in the name of King Xerxes and sealed with the king's signet ring. Dispatches were sent by swift messengers into all the provinces of the empire, giving the order that all Jews—young and old, including women and children—must be killed, slaughtered, and annihilated on a single day. This was scheduled to happen on March 7 of the next year. The property of the Jews would be given to those who killed them. A copy of this decree was to be issued as law in every province and proclaimed to all peoples, so that they would be ready to do their duty on the appointed day. At the king's command, the decree went out by swift messengers, and it was also proclaimed in the fortress of Susa. Then the king and Haman sat down to drink, but the city of Susa fell into confusion."*

Having made their agreement, the king and Haman put their plan into action, calling the secretaries to write down the fate of the Jews. The king's name and his seal authorised the decrees but it was Haman who dictated the terms of the death sentence.

King Xerxes was easy to manipulate because he was controlled by fear and greed. The king had good reason to fear for his life. We know that several years earlier Mordecai had uncovered a plot to assassinate him, but that was probably only one of many. Previously, Xerxes had shown some wisdom when he investigated to establish whether the accusation of a plot uncovered by Mordecai was true. But now, his greed was stronger than his wisdom.

It is easy for us to criticise Xerxes when we read how quickly Haman was able to manipulate him. But we need to look at ourselves and ask whether we would have acted any differently. Perhaps we would be able to reject a bribe which forced us to condemn someone else to death. But Xerxes lived in an era when a king was expected to kill his enemies. Even today, many countries put those who commit treason to death.

If we are desperate for money and are offered enough to pay for everything we want, the temptation is difficult to refuse. But, the truth is that in every bribe there is a death sentence. When we decide to take a bribe we put our faith in man instead of God. And we can only receive spiritual life when we put our faith in God alone.

A further bribe was given to anyone willing to take part in the extermination of the Jews: the land of anyone killed would become the property of the murderer. Again, Haman knew that few would be able to resist that temptation.

Today, the church in many countries accepts the bribe of their government which offers tax concessions on condition that government policy is followed. That policy includes many laws which the church should be unable to accept but does so in order to obtain the concessions.

It is helpful to realise that the decree to exterminate the Jews was very similar to the Lord's decree to King Saul to exterminate the Amalekites (1 Samuel 15:3). The two nations were destined to destroy each other. Today, we have the same calling to destroy every enemy of the Lord. The difference today is that we know our enemy is spiritual. They are the powers and authorities of darkness (Ephesians 6).

Having sent the decrees throughout the empire, the king and Haman sat down to drink, each believing that they had obtained what they wanted. They sat in a palace secure from the outside world by armed forces. But they were unaware that they had set in motion a battle with God which they could not win.

Outside the palace was confusion, starting in Susa but spreading throughout the empire. It was not just the Jews who were confused. They were not universally hated and generally had a good reputation wherever they lived. The Jews, who believed they were safe from their enemies because they were living in captivity, realised that an older foe was trying to destroy them. But there were many nations in captivity. Each one now realised that they were in as much danger as the Jews.

Our circumstances are not much different today. Much of the world lives in comparative safety. But when the plans of our enemy become known, we will realise we are in danger.

Fifteen

Esther 4:1-6 *"When Mordecai learned about all that had been done, he tore his clothes, put on burlap and ashes, and went out into the city, crying with a loud and bitter wail. He went as far as the gate of the palace, for no one was allowed to enter the palace gate while wearing clothes of mourning. And as news of the king's decree reached all the provinces, there was great mourning among the Jews. They fasted, wept, and wailed, and many people lay in burlap and ashes. When Queen Esther's maids and eunuchs came and told her about Mordecai, she was deeply distressed. She sent clothing to him to replace the burlap, but he refused it. Then Esther sent for Hathach, one of the king's eunuchs who had been appointed as her attendant. She ordered him to go to Mordecai and find out what was troubling him and why he was in mourning. So Hathach went out to Mordecai in the square in front of the palace gate."*

Because of his court position, Mordecai quickly heard about the decree of the king to destroy all Jews in the empire. His response was immediate and loud. He tore his clothes as a sign of his nakedness before God. He put on burlap, often called sackcloth, and ashes. This was often underneath outer clothing and not outwardly visible. It was uncomfortable to wear causing itching. But it was worn as a sign to God of the wearer's grief.

In addition to his importance in court circles, Mordecai was a prominent figure in the Jewish community. And news of his unusual activity and the reason for it quickly spread throughout Susa causing widespread mourning and fasting.

As no-one in mourning was allowed in the palace, Mordecai could not take his usual place at the King's gate. Esther, possibly fearing for Mordecai's safety if he disobeyed the edict about mourning in the palace, sent fresh clothes for him to wear. But he refused her offer of help.

We are not told how many Jews responded to their plight in faith towards God. Many responded by wearing burlap and with fasting which were outward signs that they sought God. But the noise of mourning which accompanied these signs suggests there was no real faith.

Today, our responses in times of difficulty are much the same. We often allow hopelessness to creep over us. We might know that fasting and prayer is the right response. But we have little faith that God will answer. Sometimes, we need an injection of faith to enable us to find peace.

Mordecai was a righteous man who believed in God's power. And as he responded to the news of the king's edict, he immediately looked for God's answer. He did not know it yet but he was an important part of the answer. He had been given a position in the empire by God in order to save His people.

Today, God is giving strategic positions to His people throughout the world. They are secular positions with no apparent connection to the Kingdom of God. But the people in those positions are connected; connected both to God and to others similarly positioned by God.

The truth is that God always has an answer to the challenges we face. Sometimes, the answer is within us. But at other times, the Lord puts others in positions to provide His answer. What God wants from us is that we trust Him with simple faith. As we have faith in Him, He might ask us to fast and pray or respond in a different way. He might simply ask us to trust Him. We need to hear Him to know how to respond.

It is not unusual for us to have periods when we wonder why we are doing what we do. At those times there seems to be little spiritual value in our activity. I wonder if Mordecai had the same doubts during his employment for the King. He was serving an ungodly man and he was doing a job which enabled the king to keep the Jews in captivity. Mordecai, like many Jews, had a passion for Jerusalem and the Temple. But he was not seeing any fruit out of that passion. And now, the king had passed an edict which would ensure Mordecai's passion could never be fulfilled.

God puts us in position for His Kingdom purposes. Are we in position yet? Sometimes God disturbs or unsettles us so that we move on from one position into another. Each time we move, whether it is our employment or our residence, we need to ensure we are in the will of God. We need to be in position for when God needs us to act.

Sixteen

Esther 4:7-9 "Mordecai told him the whole story, including the exact amount of money Haman had promised to pay into the royal treasury for the destruction of the Jews. Mordecai gave Hathach a copy of the decree issued in Susa that called for the death of all Jews. He asked Hathach to show it to Esther and explain the situation to her. He also asked Hathach to direct her to go to the king to beg for mercy and plead for her people. So Hathach returned to Esther with Mordecai's message."

When Esther heard that Mordecai was mourning she sent Hathach, one of the king's eunuchs who was attending her, to find out what was wrong. And Mordecai was able to tell the whole story, including the exact cost of the bribe. For him to know the details of the agreement between the king and Haman, Mordecai must have held an official position in the Treasury. This would also explain why he spent much time at the king's gate as that was the place where taxes and payments to the king were received.

Mordecai explained the dire situation of the Jews in detail to Hathach and asked him to give Esther a full report. In doing so, Mordecai hoped Esther would realise that her own life was in danger. But he also wanted her co-operation in a plan that was forming in his mind. He asked Esther to go to the king and beg for mercy.

The way Mordecai asked for help from Esther gives us a helpful pattern for when we make our own requests for assistance from God and people. He gave a full account of the situation leaving nothing out. He also gave a specific request concerning what he wanted Esther to do.

Because of our personal involvement in assisting Africans to begin or grow small businesses, we are often asked for assistance. To help us to decide whether to help, we will usually ask for a simple business plan so that the person wanting assistance can prove they have thought carefully about what they want to do. It is rare for anyone to give a full account of their situation. Instead, each man or woman focuses on unrealistic expectations, taking little or no account of the costs they will meet from day to day.

It is not just Africans who have unrealistic dreams. Most people are unable to assess their situation with reality. Jesus teaches us that we should always count the cost before we make decisions (Luke 14:25-35).

Mordecai knew his situation with clarity. And he hid nothing from Hathach. We often try to hide things when asking for help. And in doing so, we do not live in the light, preferring darkness. If we trusted God, we would be able to live in the light despite the difficulties we feel we need to hide.

Our honesty is important in building relationships. If we hide some important facts from a person we look to for help that relationship is not built on a good foundation. It will certainly fail until we are honest.

It is the same when we look to God for help. He expects us be honest about our situation. It is true He already knows the score. He knows everything about us. But He wants us to be honest with ourselves as well as Him. He wants us to be realistic. When we ask Him for a miracle, He expects us to know whether we have the faith to believe He will do what we ask.

Often, we come to God with empty words. We tell Him He can perform miracles but we do not believe He will do one for us. It is like the disciples when Jesus came down from the mountain after being transfigured. His disciples were trying to heal a boy of epilepsy without success. When they asked why they were unsuccessful Jesus explained it was a question of faith. We only need a small amount to move a mountain. But we have to have it, however small (Matthew 17: 14-21).

Mordecai believed Esther could change the heart of King Xerxes. But before he asked her to go to the king, Mordecai explained the situation to Hathach in detail. He then depended on Hathach to communicate his message to Esther.

Hathach was a righteous communicator, giving Esther all the details as Mordecai had requested. If he had been unrighteous or forgetful there might have been a different ending to the story of Esther. But, Hathach was diligent as a messenger.

Today, we are also called to be messengers. And the fruit of the message depends on our faithfulness in retelling it. The message is the good news of salvation to the world. Do we have a full knowledge of the message?

Seventeen

Esther 4:10-17 *"Then Esther told Hathach to go back and relay this message to Mordecai: "All the king's officials and even the people in the provinces know that anyone who appears before the king in his inner court without being invited is doomed to die unless the king holds out his gold sceptre. And the king has not called for me to come to him for thirty days." So Hathach gave Esther's message to Mordecai. Mordecai sent this reply to Esther: "Don't think for a moment that because you're in the palace you will escape when all other Jews are killed. If you keep quiet at a time like this, deliverance and relief for the Jews will arise from some other place, but you and your relatives will die. Who knows if perhaps you were made queen for just such a time as this?" Then Esther sent this reply to Mordecai: "Go and gather together all the Jews of Susa and fast for me. Do not eat or drink for three days, night or day. My maids and I will do the same. And then, though it is against the law, I will go in to see the king. If I must die, I must die." So Mordecai went away and did everything as Esther had ordered him."*

Mordecai asked Esther to appeal to the king for mercy even to the extent of begging Xerxes. This request made Esther the central figure in the salvation of the Jews. She did not baulk at playing her part. But she informed Mordecai of the dangers of his plan. She would put her life in danger if she went to the king and he did not want to see her.

Anyone who entered the king's presence when he was in his inner court would die unless the king held out his gold sceptre. This was a recognised custom and brought the king freedom from unwanted interruptions. How different this kingdom of the

Medes and Persians is to the court of heaven. We are invited to come before the presence of God with boldness and freedom. There is only one condition we have to meet: we have to be born of God. We need not fear rejection or death. He welcomes us with gladness (Hebrews 10:19-25).

The king had not called for Esther for thirty days. This might have been a sign that his love for Esther was waning making any uninvited entry into his presence even more dangerous. Mordecai listened to Hathach as he gave Esther's message but did not seek to lessen Esther's role. Instead he warned Esther that she and her family would certainly die if she did not do as he asked.

Mordecai trusted God. He knew that the Jews would be saved in one way or another. But he also knew that there would be consequences for Esther if she did not take her place in God's rescue plan. Today, we have the same choice as Esther. We also face an enemy who wants to destroy God's people. We each have a part to play in God's plan of salvation. But if we choose to opt out of our part, we will suffer the eternal consequences.

Mordecai asked Esther the rhetorical question *"Who knows if perhaps you were made queen for just such a time as this?"* It is a question often asked today. The fact is that we have each been born for such a time as this. We each have our part in God's plan and eternal purpose. Do we know what it is and will we accept it?

Esther accepted her responsibility, even though it was dangerous. But she needed God to be with her. Therefore, she asked Mordecai to gather together all the Jews in Susa in order to fast for three days. This was not the same fasting that the Jews did when they first heard about the edict for their extermination. Then it was a fast of mourning. Now it was a fast of faith.

The purpose of fasting is to purify the body and to listen to God. Esther requested that no food or drink would be consumed for three days. She wanted a purified and focussed appeal to God from His chosen people.

Today, there are many different forms of fasting. Some will fast for a day or three days and others for forty days. We might fast from food only or from certain types of food. Some fast every day only eating one meal a day. However we fast, we need to do so with faith that God will speak to us or answer our prayers.

Although Esther does not mention it, fasting is usually accompanied with prayer. The name of God is deliberately not mentioned in the book of Esther because the narrator wants us to realise that the work of God is always going on in an unseen way. Prayer is also omitted because to mention it would include God.

Having asked Mordecai to call a fast, Esther told him that she will go to the king afterwards and said *"If I must die, I must die."* In accepting her role, she accepted death. In reality, she would die whatever her choice. It would either be a physical death or the death she chose. She died to her self-government, giving herself to the will of God.

Today, we also need to die to self-government. We are called to play our part. But we can only do that effectively as we accept the will of God in our lives.

Eighteen

Esther 5:1-8 *"On the third day of the fast, Esther put on her royal robes and entered the inner court of the palace, just across from the king's hall. The king was sitting on his royal throne, facing the entrance. When he saw Queen Esther standing there in the inner court, he welcomed her and held out the gold sceptre to her. So Esther approached and touched the end of the sceptre. Then the king asked her, "What do you want, Queen Esther? What is your request? I will give it to you, even if it is half the kingdom!" And Esther replied, "If it pleases the king, let the king and Haman come today to a banquet I have prepared for the king." The king turned to his attendants and said, "Tell Haman to come quickly to a banquet, as Esther has requested." So the king and Haman went to Esther's banquet. And while they were drinking wine, the king said to Esther, "Now tell me what you really want. What is your request? I will give it to you, even if it is half the kingdom!" Esther replied, "This is my request and deepest wish. If I have found favour with the king, and if it pleases the king to grant my request and do what I ask, please come with Haman tomorrow to the banquet I will prepare for you. Then I will explain what this is all about.""*

On the third day of the fast Esther prepared for her uninvited meeting with Xerxes. She had asked her fellow Jews to fast, and many had put on sackcloth and ashes, but Esther clothed herself with her royal robes. She wanted to be as attractive as possible for the king so that he would accept her intrusion into his privacy. She also wanted him to realise she was coming to him as the queen, not just as his wife.

Today, one of Satan's objectives is to force uniformity, destroying our unique differences and callings. Even in churches, the tradition of sitting in seats to listen to a speaker or worship band gives no freedom for our unique gifts to have expression. If Esther had yielded to the pressure to conform to what she had asked of others she would have had to go to Xerxes in mourning. But she and we today, are called to a unique journey with God. We do not need to do what everyone else is doing. We need to respond to what God asks of us individually.

When Esther entered the king's inner sanctum, the king was facing the entrance doorway. This was one of those divine "coincidences" which often occur when God is in action. Probably, we can each give testimony of times when we have experienced a God-incidence.

Xerxes welcomed Esther, holding out his gold sceptre, which she touched as a sign acknowledging his royal position. We can see the faith of Esther as she walked into the king's presence. It is true that she had no choice. But we can see her confidence as she teased the king, refusing to give him the reason for her request for him and Haman to attend a banquet with her.

We have already seen the similarity between the court of Xerxes and the court of heaven. We also are invited into the presence of God to speak with Him. Like Esther, we can be bold as we approach God. If we have been made righteous through our faith in the sacrifice of Jesus, He welcomes us to make our requests boldly to Him (Heb 4:16).

Having been accepted as king by Esther touching his gold sceptre, King Xerxes addressed Esther as his queen. This was not just a conversation between a husband and wife; it was between the king and queen. And it immediately became more significant.

Xerxes continued to talk on the basis of being king, offering Esther up to half his kingdom. Although that offer was a traditional greeting, Xerxes demonstrated his trust in Esther by using it. If Xerxes, a pagan king, could be so generous to Esther, how much more generous is God to us when we approach Him? He does not offer us half a kingdom. He gives us the whole kingdom if we seek Him for it.

Three times Xerxes asked Esther what she wanted from him. But Esther was not ready to tell him. She wanted the full three days of the fast to be completed before she told Xerxes what she really wanted. Instead, she asked Xerxes and Haman to attend a banquet the following day.

If Esther had told Xerxes what she really wanted immediately she would have spoken too quickly and events would not have followed the course they did. The delay was vital for God's plan to be outworked.

Today, we also need to learn how to control our tongues. When we share the good news of the Kingdom of God with people, we need to be sensitive what we share and how we do so. There is little point in talking about difficult subjects until someone has the faith to hear it. We need to learn patience. But above all else, we need to learn to be sensitive to what Holy Spirit is saying.

Nineteen

Esther 5:5-8 *"The king turned to his attendants and said, "Tell Haman to come quickly to a banquet, as Esther has requested." So the king and Haman went to Esther's banquet. And while they were drinking wine, the king said to Esther, "Now tell me what you really want. What is your request? I will give it to you, even if it is half the kingdom!" Esther replied, "This is my request and deepest wish. If I have found favour with the king, and if it pleases the king to grant my request and do what I ask, please come with Haman tomorrow to the banquet I will prepare for you. Then I will explain what this is all about.""*

When we read about the response of Xerxes to Esther we realise that God responds quickly to us when we set our faces to seek Him with prayer and fasting. Despite having no time for her in the previous thirty days, Xerxes welcomed Esther. He offered her half his kingdom. He willingly acquiesced to all her demands. He was a man who was used to people doing everything he wanted immediately. Yet when Esther refused to tell him her real motives, he patiently waited as she requested.

When we approach God, He looks for our faith and expectancy. When He finds what is in our heart, He responds in like measures. If He finds faith, He meets us at our point of faith. If He finds doubt and unbelief, He can give us nothing. It is a spiritual law which God obeys.

Esther invited her enemy, Haman, to a banquet. She was not afraid of him despite the political power he had to have her killed. At the banquet she plied him with food and wine, holding nothing back as she entertained him and the king. She did not reveal her natural anger and antagonism to him, keeping her true feelings under control.

Today, we can also live among people who are our enemies. Not everyone will like us because personality clashes frequently occur. It is even possible that we will not like someone else. As we grow in spiritual maturity we will learn how to love even when we feel unloving. Our feelings of dislike come from our old nature, a nature which has a root of hate. As we grow in God, we learn how to overcome in the battle against hate.

As they were drinking, the king again asked Esther to reveal her true motives. But she evaded the question by requesting the king and Haman attend another banquet, postponing her answer until the following day. Esther tested the king to see whether he really meant what he said by couching her invitation to another banquet with the condition *"If I have found favour with the king, and if it pleases the king to grant my request and do what I ask".* In doing so, she was asking Xerxes to agree to what she wanted before he heard what it was.

This is a common tactic today when someone wants an agreement before revealing the terms of the agreement. For example, someone will say *"Will you promise me something?"* And in doing so the person is toying with the emotions of the individual being manipulated. When someone asks that question we are wise to wait until we know what is being asked before promising anything!

Xerxes did not hesitate in promising Esther what she asked, agreeing to attend another banquet the following day. This was the third time the king had agreed to something without knowing the conditions. The first occasion was when Haman had asked him to sign the death warrant for the Jews. The other times were when Esther asked him to attend a banquet. On each occasion, the king was ultimately agreeing to the destruction of many people.

The truth is that our words and actions are never insignificant. Jesus taught that what comes out of our mouths reveals what is in our hearts. And our actions reveal our decisions. James taught that the tongue is like a small rudder which steers a large ship (James 3:1-12). And what the tongue says can start world wars.

Esther used her words to obtain what she wanted. When we analyse what she said, we realise she was manipulating Xerxes, using her feminine charms to persuade him to agree with her. It is not a technique we would advocate today. In fact, many would criticise her, accusing her of having a "Jezebel spirit". Xerxes, although ruthless, like Ahab was weak in character.

But Esther was not the same as Jezebel. Esther trusted the Lord, not a foreign god. Esther acted in faith. And the Lord responded to that faith inciting Xerxes to do all that Esther wanted.

Today, the Lord still looks at our heart, responding to our faith. We are called to be warriors in His army and He wants us to enjoy the fight. We will often be outnumbered and outwitted. But we are on the Lord's side. As we trust Him and respond in faith to all He says, we will win.

Twenty

Esther 5:9-14 *"Haman was a happy man as he left the banquet! But when he saw Mordecai sitting at the palace gate, not standing up or trembling nervously before him, Haman became furious. However, he restrained himself and went on home. Then Haman gathered together his friends and Zeresh, his wife, and boasted to them about his great wealth and his many children. He bragged about the honours the king had given him and how he had been promoted over all the other nobles and officials. Then Haman added, "And that's not all! Queen Esther invited only me and the king himself to the banquet she prepared for us. And she has invited me to dine with her and the king again tomorrow!" Then he added, "But this is all worth nothing as long as I see Mordecai the Jew just sitting there at the palace gate." So Haman's wife, Zeresh, and all his friends suggested, "Set up a sharpened pole that stands seventy-five feet tall, and in the morning ask the king to impale Mordecai on it. When this is done, you can go on your merry way to the banquet with the king." This pleased Haman, and he ordered the pole set up."*

Haman was a happy man when he left Esther's banquet, thinking he had been highly honoured by both the king and the queen. His emotions were soaring. This is a salutary lesson to us that we should never rely on our feelings to understand our situation. We need to live from our spirit, listening to the voice of God, who always speaks truth.

There are times when we feel down and discouraged, fearful of the outcome of a particular challenge. But when we come through to the other side we find that the thing we fear never happens. We need to encourage ourselves at all times. We do this by reading and believing the words of God. The easiest way to do this is to read the bible and listen as Spirit God makes the words real to us. But we can find encouragement in many places such as listening to people we trust as well as to God directly. If we have ears to hear Him, the voice of God can be heard in the most unlikely places.

Shortly after Haman left the banquet he saw Mordecai sitting at the King's gate. And Haman's emotions again controlled his life sending him into a furious rage. Ironically, previously Haman had been angry that Mordecai did not bow before him. But now he is angry because, Mordecai did not stand. The truth is that hatred causes us to be irrational in our responses.

Haman boasted about many things to his wife and friends. He had acquired much wealth. He also had 10 children and large families were considered to be a great blessing in his culture. He also boasted about his position in the empire and his favour to be invited to another feast. His boasting was about material benefits. He had nothing of eternal value to boast about.

There are many people today who boast about the things they have acquired, comparing their importance to others on the basis of their wealth. It is a foolish boast because everything we own and all that we do will be "burnt up" to test its eternal value (1 Corinthians 3:10-15). This is probably not a physical burning. Instead, it is a picture of the trials we go through to assess whether we are building our life on the foundation of Jesus. The only thing worth boasting about is what God has done and is doing in our lives (Galatians 6:14).

Haman could not forget his hatred of Mordecai. And even when he was boasting about his wealth, his children and the favour he had received, he remembered that Mordecai would not submit to him. His wife and friends had a solution, suggesting he set up a sharpened pole, seventy-five feet tall, on which to impale Mordecai.

If the measurement is right, this was a long pole! But perhaps it was a more regular sized pole raised up to the height recorded by being on a hill or on the walls of the city. The height itself is not too important. What is important is the hatred which Haman felt which forced him to want to make an exhibition of Mordecai which the whole city would see.

If we allow it, our feelings lead us to do things we regret. When we are happy we will be unusually generous, giving away all that we own. When we are fearful we will not take steps of faith which would lead us into the purposes of God. When we are in a bad mood we will be rude and spiteful to others. None of these things are good behaviour for a man or woman of God.

The truth is that God has feelings also. Jesus demonstrated this when He ministered the love of God for three and a half years before He went to His cross. He laughed and cried as He responded to the emotions of His Father. And we also need to learn how to feel the emotions of the Spirit. To do that we first need to put to death our old nature. When we no longer rely on our old emotions we can learn to feel as God feels.

Twenty one

Esther 6:1-3 *"That night the king had trouble sleeping, so he ordered an attendant to bring the book of the history of his reign so it could be read to him. In those records he discovered an account of how Mordecai had exposed the plot of Bigthana and Teresh, two of the eunuchs who guarded the door to the king's private quarters. They had plotted to assassinate King Xerxes. "What reward or recognition did we ever give Mordecai for this?" the king asked. His attendants replied, "Nothing has been done for him.""*

It was when the situation looked most impossible for His people that God responded to their fasting and prayer. When we read the story, it seems as if God and Esther choreographed their actions to interact at precisely the right moment. Esther invited Xerxes and Haman to a banquet to be held the day after God gave the king a restless night, a night in which he remembered the good deeds of Mordecai.

It is possible that Esther contrived the events of the night. She might have arranged for food which gave Xerxes a restless night. She might have asked the attendant to give him the record of Mordecai's act of loyalty to the king. Although it is possible that Esther was the unseen hand behind Xerxes night, it is highly improbable. A more accurate and simpler explanation is that God was responding to His people. It was God who allowed the circumstances to unravel as they did.

The fact is that Esther had a plan which she would reveal at the banquet the following day. It was a bold plan which could easily backfire and cause even more hardship to her and her people.

But God knew that plan. He always knows what we think. And God ensured that Esther's plan would be accepted by the king.

When we face challenges and ask the Lord to help us, we do not know how He will respond. Sometimes the situation is impossible with no apparent solution. There is nothing we can do except trust the Lord in faith. Often, we turn to the Lord in our desperation but we do not really expect Him to help. Even then, He can surprise us giving unexpected deliverance. But when we have learned to trust Him; when we have experienced His help, He expects us to grow in faith.

Every challenge we face is a gift from God. It is an opportunity to grow in faith. The writers of the New Testament encourage us to be excited when we have challenges. They knew that God always gave them a way through the challenge. The truth is that God allows the difficulties in order to help us to grow in faith and spiritual maturity (James 1:2-4; 1 Peter 1:6-9; Romans 5:3-5). We can see that Esther had that kind of faith. She was not in mourning and hopelessness when she spoke to the king. She was wearing her royal robes, just as we should wear our royal robes as we go through each trial.

We do not know how God will answer our prayers. But we can be confident that He will answer them.

Xerxes was restless during the night and wanted someone to read a book to him so that he could go to sleep. The book he requested was a record of his achievements during his reign. Xerxes seems to have been an insecure person and his choice of reading material infers that he wanted to boost his ego. Today, when we face our challenges, it is always helpful to remind ourselves how the Lord has helped us in the past.

By "coincidence" the attendant read the events of Mordecai's loyalty. Xerxes, following the culture of the Medes and Persians who believed in rewarding good deeds, asked how Mordecai had been rewarded and was told that nothing had been done.

We are not told how Mordecai felt about the way his action to save the life of Xerxes had been forgotten. Today, we also like to give recognition to those who deserve it. And if we do not receive recognition for our actions we tend to became discouraged. An employee who works harder than others expects a larger pay rise. If the pay rise is not given the employee often leaves the company. A wife who serves her husband well can expect to be loved in return. But if that love is not evident, she will become discouraged and feel rejected.

The truth is that our life belongs to the Lord and we live to serve Him. It is better for us if we look for any reward to come from Him, not from men or women. God promises that He will reward us according to our lives. He does not tell us when that reward will be given. Sometimes, that reward might be in this life and last for a short while only. But often, we do not receive our reward until we pass through death into the next stage of life. In that case, our reward lasts for eternity.

Providentially, Mordecai had not been rewarded for his actions. Xerxes now felt compelled to do something to rectify that omission.

Twenty two

Ester 6:4-9 ""*Who is that in the outer court?" the king inquired. As it happened, Haman had just arrived in the outer court of the palace to ask the king to impale Mordecai on the pole he had prepared. So the attendants replied to the king, "Haman is out in the court." "Bring him in," the king ordered. So Haman came in, and the king said, "What should I do to honour a man who truly pleases me?" Haman thought to himself, "Whom would the king wish to honour more than me?" So he replied, "If the king wishes to honour someone, he should bring out one of the king's own royal robes, as well as a horse that the king himself has ridden—one with a royal emblem on its head. Let the robes and the horse be handed over to one of the king's most noble officials. And let him see that the man whom the king wishes to honour is dressed in the king's robes and led through the city square on the king's horse. Have the official shout as they go, 'This is what the king does for someone he wishes to honour!'* ""

Having listened to the account of the unrewarded exploits of Mordecai, Xerxes heard Haman arrive. Haman's intention was to ask the king to impale Mordecai on the pole he had erected. This is another significant "coincidence" found in the story of Esther. There were many people living in the palace and many more wanting an audience with the king. But it was Haman who arrived at the opportune time.

Whilst Satan had been stirring up hatred in Haman, God was bringing Xerxes to a place of contrition for not rewarding Mordecai. The arrival of Haman, who was the king's trusted advisor, enabled Xerxes to immediately deal with the problem he had discovered about the failure to reward Mordecai.

Previously, when Haman had asked the king to sign the death warrant for the Jews, he had not disclosed the name of the people to die. Now, when the king asked Haman how he should honour Mordecai, he did not disclose Mordecai's name. We are not told whether this was a deliberate act to deceive Haman but it is unlikely that the king would be ignorant about Haman's feud with Mordecai. Therefore, the omission would be necessary for the king to obtain an unbiased recommendation from Haman.

A similar technique is often used today in ungodly negotiations. The participants do not give full information to their opponents in order to maintain a "bargaining position". Although there can always be exceptions to the rule, we should act differently when we are on Kingdom business. We are sons and daughters of the light and should live open and honest lives.

We have already seen that Haman was controlled by his emotions. His greed, lust for power and hatred of Mordecai had driven him until he no longer had the ability to see beyond his selfish desires. Now, when the king said he wanted to honour someone, Haman, in his arrogance, assumed he was that person.

Today, if we do not die to our emotional strongholds, we also will be controlled by them. Our emotions are under the control of our old nature, a nature which is a servant of Satan. Our freedom from that nature comes as we are baptised in water and start to acknowledge the Lordship of Jesus in our life. As we are led by Holy Spirit the power of our old nature is broken.

Haman answered the king on the assumption it was he who was being honoured and exposed his lust for recognition in his reply. In many ways, Haman's suggestions were an attempt to become even more powerful than he was already. In the culture, the king's robes were given mystical powers. And anyone who wore the robes assumed the king's power and stature. It was similar with the king's horse and royal emblem. Haman had already been given the royal seal. Now he wanted to have the full experience of being king.

We could argue that Haman was not being too greedy because he did not ask for money. In fact his suggestions flattered the king because they recognised the king's importance. But the reality is that Haman already had enough money. He wanted more power.

What Haman sought from the worldly king Xerxes is a picture of what is freely available to any child of God today. And we do not have to manipulate God to obtain it either. It is part of our God-given calling. We are called to reign with Christ over all creation. We live in a world which is destined to be the home of the Kingdom of God. And today we are being trained to reign with Christ in this world. We will not rule like king Xerxes, with fear and control. Instead, we are learning to reign with love and freedom as we submit to Holy Spirit.

Many teach that we will not reign until Jesus returns to earth. But the truth is that we need to be able to reign before Jesus returns. We are being trained today so that we are ready for His return. Like John the Baptist we are called to prepare the way of the Lord *"He is a voice shouting in the wilderness, 'Prepare the way for the LORD's coming! Clear the road for him! The valleys will be filled, and the mountains and hills made level. The curves will be straightened, and the rough places made smooth. And then all people will see the salvation sent from God.'"* (Isaiah 40:3)

Twenty three

Esther 6:10-14 *""Excellent!" the king said to Haman. "Quick! Take the robes and my horse, and do just as you have said for Mordecai the Jew, who sits at the gate of the palace. Leave out nothing you have suggested!" So Haman took the robes and put them on Mordecai, placed him on the king's own horse, and led him through the city square, shouting, "This is what the king does for someone he wishes to honour!" Afterward Mordecai returned to the palace gate, but Haman hurried home dejected and completely humiliated. When Haman told his wife, Zeresh, and all his friends what had happened, his wise advisers and his wife said, "Since Mordecai—this man who has humiliated you—is of Jewish birth, you will never succeed in your plans against him. It will be fatal to continue opposing him." While they were still talking, the king's eunuchs arrived and quickly took Haman to the banquet Esther had prepared."*

Having accepted Haman's advice concerning the best way for the king to honour a person, Xerxes ordered Haman to honour Mordecai following his suggestions in every detail. We can imagine how Haman's emotions responded. His greed, his pride, his hatred and his lust for power were each frustrated by the king.

The fact that Xerxes knew that Mordecai sat at the gate to the palace suggests that the king also knew about the hatred Haman felt for Mordecai. It is also probable that Haman, who could not control his emotions, showed his surprise and displeasure to the king when he heard who was to be honoured.

Despite his obvious disagreement with him, Haman could not refuse to obey the king. Any refusal would be considered treason and would result in certain death.

Today, like Haman, we might still be controlled by our emotions but it is not what God intends for us. He offers us freedom from the control of Satan's temptations. Our freedom can come in a series of steps. Firstly, during our baptism in water, our old nature, including the control of emotions, is stripped of its spiritual power. Before we are baptised, there is a spiritual law which gives Satan authority and control over us. But through baptism, a higher spiritual law takes precedence and Satan's authority is legally broken. We become free to choose who we will serve and free to decide to control our emotions.

If we continue to allow our emotions to control us, God allows circumstances to change us. We will go through challenges which test our emotions, enabling us to realise we are not yet free. If we are wise, we ask Holy Spirit to release His love and His character to replace our old nature.

Haman rejected God's love. Having honoured Mordecai, he hurried home to his wife and advisers feeling dejected and humiliated. His wife was named Zeresh, meaning "gold or misery". Her name probably enshrines her character which had joined with Haman's to seek power and wealth. She and his wise advisers seem to have realised that Haman could not win his war and could only advise that Haman stopped planning to destroy Mordecai.

The wise advisers couched their advice in the fact that Mordecai was a Jew and that Haman could never succeed against him because of his nationality. They finally realised that the God of the Jews was fighting for His people. They knew that Haman could not win.

Do we realise today that we cannot lose the war against Satan? We might lose a battle occasionally. But we will finally win the war. I write at a time when the world is in the middle of the Covid-19 pandemic. At the same time wealthy people talk publicly about the need for a world reset which would result in the loss of many lives because the greed of man has caused food and resources to be scarce. It is believed that the world's largest Companies and politicians are pursuing a one-nation mandate to usher in a new world order. The consequence of these pursuits would be to annihilate the people of God.

The battle ahead is similar to the one faced by Mordecai and Esther. But we need not be discouraged. God sits in the heavens and laughs at His enemies (Psalms 2:4-6). He still responds to His faithful people who turn to Him with prayer and fasting.

As Haman listened to his advisers, the king's eunuchs arrived to take him to Esther's banquet. It was normal for the king to send his eunuchs to accompany honoured guests to a banquet. Therefore Haman would think he was again being honoured. His depression might have lifted temporarily. But again he will find that his emotions were not speaking the truth to him.

It is another provocation to us to learn that the emotions of our old nature cannot be trusted.

Twenty four

Esther 7:1-7a *"So the king and Haman went to Queen Esther's banquet. On this second occasion, while they were drinking wine, the king again said to Esther, "Tell me what you want, Queen Esther. What is your request? I will give it to you, even if it is half the kingdom!" Queen Esther replied, "If I have found favour with the king, and if it pleases the king to grant my request, I ask that my life and the lives of my people will be spared. For my people and I have been sold to those who would kill, slaughter, and annihilate us. If we had merely been sold as slaves, I could remain quiet, for that would be too trivial a matter to warrant disturbing the king." "Who would do such a thing?" King Xerxes demanded. "Who would be so presumptuous as to touch you?" Esther replied, "This wicked Haman is our adversary and our enemy." Haman grew pale with fright before the king and queen. Then the king jumped to his feet in a rage and went out into the palace garden."*

Despite the fact that Mordecai had been publicly honoured, he and the Jews continued to face extinction because the edict of the king had not been annulled. Haman had been humiliated. But he had not yet lost his war to destroy his enemy. Therefore, he attended Esther's banquet with mixed emotions. He had lost a skirmish. But he still expected to win the war.

Today, as we fight our spiritual battles, we also need to keep our vision fixed on the end goal. Our enemy, Satan, intends to destroy our faith, as well as any worship of God. Our goal is to bring freedom to as many as possible from the kingdom of darkness which currently holds them captive. In the end, after the great harvest, we will see the kingdom of darkness destroyed.

During the second banquet the king again asked Esther the reason for her invitations for him and Haman to eat with her. This time she finally told him.

There is always a best time to act. If we move too early or too late we will miss the best time. A good comedian understands the importance of timing. The punch-line to a joke will fall flat if it is presented at the wrong time. But, when someone knows how to keep the audience in suspense for just the right time before providing the final surprise, they will be rewarded by genuine laughter. As she responded patiently to the leading of the Holy Spirit, Esther spoke at the right time.

Esther knew she had found favour with the king because he repeatedly complied with her wishes. Even so, she couched her request in terms which continued to give Xerxes the freedom to give or refuse her request. The king had signed the edict to destroy the Jews but this was the right time to acknowledge that she also was a Jew.

As she spoke, Esther acknowledged that it was in the king's interests to keep the Jews as slaves. But, contrary to his interests, the Jews were destined for death. She even accepted the position as a slave for herself and her race. However, she politely suggested that death would harm the king's interests and was unnecessary. Esther's submissive spirit to her husband, the king, as she accepted he had the right to do what he decided for her and her people shows an amazing self restraint. It is true that she had no choice in the matter but many wives, or husbands, in a similar situation would seek to manipulate their spouse far more fiercely.

Xerxes responded to Esther's disclosure with surprise and anger that anyone would seek to harm her. He was not concerned about the Jews generally. Their death was not important to him. He was only concerned and angry that his wife, his queen, was threatened. His response shows how he was totally absorbed with himself.

Up to this moment, Haman seems to be unaware that it was his plan which was being disclosed. But, when Esther exposed Haman as her enemy, he paled. He finally realised that his life was itself threatened.

At this point Xerxes, surprisingly, went out to the palace gardens to compose himself leaving Haman and Esther together. He had never bothered to even try to control his emotions previously. It might have helped him to calm down if he had questioned Esther's story to establish its validity but he accepted what she had told him. He would almost certainly have remembered Haman's previous trickery. In any event, he had not questioned many previous reports he had received.

He is not named, but we can see God's hand in all the events which led to the exposure of Haman. Today, although we live in a time when the plans of darkness seem to be winning the war between good and evil, we need not be discouraged. God is also at work behind the scenes, unseen and often unknown. As we seek Him, He will expose the works of darkness. His Kingdom will continue to grow until every part of the world is full of His glorious people.

Twenty five

Esther 7:7b-10 *"Haman, however, stayed behind to plead for his life with Queen Esther, for he knew that the king intended to kill him. In despair he fell on the couch where Queen Esther was reclining, just as the king was returning from the palace garden. The king exclaimed, "Will he even assault the queen right here in the palace, before my very eyes?" And as soon as the king spoke, his attendants covered Haman's face, signalling his doom. Then Harbona, one of the king's eunuchs, said, "Haman has set up a sharpened pole that stands seventy-five feet tall in his own courtyard. He intended to use it to impale Mordecai, the man who saved the king from assassination." "Then impale Haman on it!" the king ordered. So they impaled Haman on the pole he had set up for Mordecai, and the king's anger subsided."*

In the short time it took Esther to reveal his plan, Haman finally realised that his life was coming to an end. And he took the opportunity to plead for mercy to Queen Esther, knowing that she was the only person who could appeal to the king to spare him.

It was normal practice for intimate meals to be eaten whilst lying on individual couches. The food would either be served by the attendants or left on a low table for self service. In his despair, Haman left his couch and fell onto the one used by Esther, seeking to be nearer to her as he pled for his life. It was his last error of judgement because Xerxes returned at that moment to witness his apparent assault on his queen.

The attendants watching the scene were quick to cover Haman's face so that the king need see him no longer; much like a judge in more modern times would cover his own head with a black cloth when proclaiming the death sentence.

Harbona, one of the king's eunuchs who clearly did not like Haman, revealed how Haman had set up the long pole to impale Mordecai. He added that Mordecai was the man who had saved the king's life, emphasising the accuracy of Esther's account. The king made a typically spontaneous decision to impale Haman on the pole instead.

Haman had a short time only to remember his shortcomings before his life ended. We are not told how he used that short time. Sadly, his hatred for Mordecai and the Jews probably stopped him from repenting for his sins. In fact, he probably thought his hatred was justified. It is a sad fact that we rarely can see our faults. And we take great pains in order to justify our decisions and actions.

Haman had only himself to blame for his early death. He spent his life in rebellion to God and seeking to destroy God's people. There are many today who rebel against God, often without realising the fact. For Haman, his rebellion started in the cultural issue that Israel was a sworn enemy. He was born into rebellion.

Today, our culture has a similar hold on us. Our children are frequently taught in schools that God's laws are not right. Cultural role models declare that God does not exist. And because of these things the "Haman spirit" of rebellion and pride is rampant in society.

Throughout Esther's banquet, Mordecai and the Jewish population throughout the Empire were unaware how events were developing. Through this we can be encouraged that we do not always see how God is answering our prayers. He works in ways which we do not understand. And His answers can come from a surprising source and in an impossible way.

Even after Haman had been impaled on his pole, the Jews faced an uncertain future. They had won a battle and their chief adversary was dead. But their death sentence still stood. It was not the time to stop praying.

It is much the same for us today. We can be tempted to rest after we achieve a victory, small or great. The battle has been tiring and we feel we must rest. It is true that we can become tired and need physical and spiritual rejuvenation. But even in that time, we remain in the war. We are called to fight until the war is over.

Twenty six

Esther 8:1-2 *"On that same day King Xerxes gave the property of Haman, the enemy of the Jews, to Queen Esther. Then Mordecai was brought before the king, for Esther had told the king how they were related. The king took off his signet ring—which he had taken back from Haman—and gave it to Mordecai. And Esther appointed Mordecai to be in charge of Haman's property."*

On the same day that Haman was impaled on the pole he had erected to kill Mordecai, the king gave Esther Haman's property. We saw earlier that Esther had limited her request to Xerxes for him to spare her life and the lives of the Jews, not even asking for freedom from slavery. But Xerxes responded to her by giving much more than she had requested. He made her one of the wealthiest people in the Empire.

After ensuring Esther was rightly rewarded for her faithfulness, Xerxes honoured Mordecai again. He had already honoured him by parading Mordecai on the king's horse whilst wearing the king's robes. He now honoured him to be the most powerful man in the empire after the king. Xerxes had already recovered his signet ring from Haman. He now gave that ring to Mordecai, giving him the authority to speak and act in the name of the king.

Mordecai had a further honour entrusted to him when Esther appointed him to be in charge of Haman's property. He was now responsible for both public affairs as second in command to the king and also of the largest private properties in the empire. He had been promoted in every area of his life.

Today, we also can expect promotions in the Kingdom of God when we engage in the war against evil. A promotion comes with a test. Usually the test comes before the promotion but it is also possible for the test to challenge the promotion. Esther was promoted to be queen before her test so that she was in position for the test. Mordecai was promoted after successfully overcoming the test. It is also true that there would not have been a test at all if Mordecai had not received his initial promotion which caused him to sit in the king's gate where he caught the eye of Haman.

We should never expect the Christian life to be without challenges. We read in Acts *"After preaching the Good News in Derbe and making many disciples, Paul and Barnabas returned to Lystra, Iconium, and Antioch of Pisidia, where they strengthened the believers. They encouraged them to continue in the faith, reminding them that we must suffer many hardships to enter the Kingdom of God."* (Acts 14:21-22) With the challenges God gives His joy and peace. He encourages us by giving faith. He promises to never leave us. But He expects us to go through the difficulties.

With each challenge comes the opportunity to overcome. And when we overcome we gain spiritual ground which the enemy loses. We also gain the rewards offered to those who overcome; rewards which are geared towards specific challenges. Some of those rewards are described in Revelation 1-2, although Paul adds more in his writings.

Mordecai received an obvious tangible reward. His faithfulness to God as well as to Xerxes was rewarded by wealth and power. He had sought for neither of these things. His only motive was to be honourable and to live righteously. It is the same for us today. We do not need to seek wealth and power. These are in the hands of God and He will give these things to those He rewards. In reality, it is better to grow in spirit than it is to receive a tangible reward.

God rewards faithfulness. He sees all that we do and think. We might be able to hide from men and women but we cannot hide from Him. And He seeks those whom He can reward. When we are faithful in little things, He promotes us so that we can be faithful in bigger ones. If we are faithful with the world's wealth, God will entrust us with His kingdom. If we are faithful with the things of others, God will give us our own things (Luke 16:10-13).

Despite their rewards, Esther and Mordecai still faced the greater challenge of the extermination of the Jews. But they had been promoted and were now in a position to fight their next battle.

Twenty seven

Esther 8:3-8 *"Then Esther went again before the king, falling down at his feet and begging him with tears to stop the evil plot devised by Haman the Agagite against the Jews. Again the king held out the gold sceptre to Esther. So she rose and stood before him. Esther said, "If it please the king, and if I have found favour with him, and if he thinks it is right, and if I am pleasing to him, let there be a decree that reverses the orders of Haman son of Hammedatha the Agagite, who ordered that Jews throughout all the king's provinces should be destroyed. For how can I endure to see my people and my family slaughtered and destroyed?" Then King Xerxes said to Queen Esther and Mordecai the Jew, "I have given Esther the property of Haman, and he has been impaled on a pole because he tried to destroy the Jews. Now go ahead and send a message to the Jews in the king's name, telling them whatever you want, and seal it with the king's signet ring. But remember that whatever has already been written in the king's name and sealed with his signet ring can never be revoked.""*

Again Esther puts her life at risk by going to the king without his prior consent. She was now a wealthy landowner in her own right having taken possession of Haman's property. Yet she acknowledged Xerxes' authority over her as she fell at his feet, begging him to stop the destruction of the Jews.

Esther did not become proud in her wealth. She continued to submit to Xerxes with humility. True humility comes when we know that we can do nothing of value in our own strength but that we can do anything through Christ who strengthens us. Esther knew that her newly gained wealth and status could not save her or her people against the finality of the Law of the Medes and Persians.

Today we face the same conclusion. Our wealth, worldly position and physical strength cannot save us from the eternal Law of God passed when Satan tempted man to rebel in the Garden of Eden. Sin is rebellion against God. Sin is making our decisions without God. And the wages of sin is spiritual death. We cannot buy spiritual life with our money. We cannot bully God with our power. Like Esther, we can only fall at the feet of God asking Him for mercy.

Again the king held out his gold sceptre to Esther welcoming her to share her concerns with him. It is the same for us as we fall in faith and repentance at the feet of God. He welcomes us into His confidence.

Esther gave four conditions to Xerxes, each one providing him with the opportunity to reject her. Firstly, the king had to want to do what she asked. The decision had to be from the king. Secondly, Esther had to have found favour with the king. He had to take action on the basis that he loved Esther. Thirdly, the king had to agree that his action was the right one. And lastly, Esther asked the king to act on the basis that he was pleased with her. This is different from the second condition. We might love someone but not be pleased with their actions. Xerxes answered immediately telling Esther how to resolve the situation. All conditions were fully met.

Today, when we come to God with our petitions, it is helpful to give Him the same conditions. Does God want to do what we ask? If we ask according to His will, He will always act. Do we find favour with God? We can only come to Him on the basis that Jesus has taken our punishment. If we have faith in what

Jesus has done, God accepts us. Is the action we ask from God right? If we ask Him to do something immoral or unrighteous, we cannot expect Him to agree. Is He pleased by our actions?

The king told Esther to take whatever action she wanted using the signet ring he had given to Mordecai. There was only one condition he made: previous laws could not be overturned. We have the same condition as we meet with God. His spiritual laws cannot be overturned. The wages of sin are always spiritual death. But, God passed a new law when Jesus paid our debt on the cross. We can now escape spiritual death by faith in the work of Jesus.

There are times today when God gives us permission to do what we want in response to our petition to Him. At other times He asks us to stand still while He acts on our behalf. There are occasions when He gives us clear guidance on a course of action. When God says nothing, He asks us to trust Him. Sometimes, the conditions have not been met and we need to repent of our attitudes. But God always hears. He is not deaf.

Twenty eight

Esther 8:9-14 *"So on June 25 the king's secretaries were summoned, and a decree was written exactly as Mordecai dictated. It was sent to the Jews and to the highest officers, the governors, and the nobles of all the 127 provinces stretching from India to Ethiopia. The decree was written in the scripts and languages of all the peoples of the empire, including that of the Jews. The decree was written in the name of King Xerxes and sealed with the king's signet ring. Mordecai sent the dispatches by swift messengers, who rode fast horses especially bred for the king's service. The king's decree gave the Jews in every city authority to unite to defend their lives. They were allowed to kill, slaughter, and annihilate anyone of any nationality or province who might attack them or their children and wives, and to take the property of their enemies. The day chosen for this event throughout all the provinces of King Xerxes was March 7 of the next year. A copy of this decree was to be issued as law in every province and proclaimed to all peoples, so that the Jews would be ready to take revenge on their enemies on the appointed day. So urged on by the king's command, the messengers rode out swiftly on fast horses bred for the king's service. The same decree was also proclaimed in the fortress of Susa."*

Finally, a plan to deliver the Jews was put into action. Although Haman's original plan to destroy Israel could not be cancelled, a new plan to empower all Jews in the Empire to defend themselves was authorised by the king's seal.

The plan had to be delivered throughout the Empire. And to ensure there were no mistakes, it was clearly written in as many languages as possible. When it was received in a district, the decree would have been publicly announced by the "Town Crier" and a copy posted on a public notice board for those who could read.

Today, we would be able to send an urgent message throughout the world in seconds using the web. But the Jews anxiously waiting for salvation were dependent on the speed and stamina of the horses. Their message of salvation often required many days in the saddle.

The plan was simple. All Jews could defend themselves against any person who sought to harm them on March 7th; the day that Haman had decreed was to be the day of slaughter.

This was not going to be an easy victory for the Jews. They had to actively fight for their lives. They could not look back on the previous times of salvation and watch God fighting on their behalf such as the day when they left Egypt and the Egyptian army was destroyed by the sea or when Jehoshaphat was delivered by an angel who slaughtered his enemies.

Today, when we are faced with a challenge, we are tempted to turn to the bible verses which promise us the easiest victory. And we place our hope in what God has done in the past. But God does not respond to us in the ways we expect. He wants us to grow in spirit and become mature. He will usually expect us to fight the enemy in order to obtain the necessary victory.

We do not fight with the physical weapons the Jews used in the days of Mordecai and Esther, although we still have the weapons of prayer and fasting. Our greatest weapon is listening to what God says. He will give the battle orders.

Our battles today often require patience and determination. God values patience highly. It is a tool He uses to develop our character.

Mordecai gave the Jews time to prepare for their day of salvation. They had opportunity to prepare their defences and develop local plans to overcome their enemies. They needed to be ready for the day when Haman's edict would be enacted by those who hated them.

We also need to be ready in our day for our battles. God trains us through the small challenges we face until we are ready for the larger ones. We should not waste the opportunities He gives to learn how to overcome our enemy.

Twenty nine

Esther 8:15-17 *"Then Mordecai left the king's presence, wearing the royal robe of blue and white, the great crown of gold, and an outer cloak of fine linen and purple. And the people of Susa celebrated the new decree. The Jews were filled with joy and gladness and were honoured everywhere. In every province and city, wherever the king's decree arrived, the Jews rejoiced and had a great celebration and declared a public festival and holiday. And many of the people of the land became Jews themselves, for they feared what the Jews might do to them. "*

Having passed the decree to allow all Jews to defend themselves against their enemies, Mordecai left the king's presence. He continued to wear the king's robes and crown giving obvious evidence that he carried the king's pleasure.

We continue to see a parallel in the relationship which Mordecai now enjoyed with the king to our own relationship with God. Mordecai had so much favour that he was allowed to wear the king's robes and crown. We also can enjoy favour with God. He gives us His robes of righteousness to wear and places a royal crown on our heads to confirm we are His sons and daughters. However, there is a difference between our relationship with God and the one Mordecai had with Xerxes. Our relationship is permanent; his only lasted a few years.

The new decree was received with great gladness throughout the Empire, commencing in Susa and growing whenever the couriers reached a new territory. It is obvious that the Jews were not hated by many. Instead, they had developed good relationships in the lands in which they had been enslaved. Now they were honoured everywhere.

It is possible the new place of honour for the Jews was granted because Mordecai was obviously now a favourite of the king. But it is equally possible that the Jews were well liked already. There are many examples of the way they were able to positively contribute into the cultures where they lived, some rising to become key figures in the political and economic scenes.

As we apply the story of Esther to our lives, we can ask the question "Are we honoured by the people around us?" It is a challenging question. When Paul wrote to both Timothy and Titus many years after the lives of Esther and Mordecai, he gave certain conditions before they should recognise the contribution of mature Christians. One of those conditions was that the person should be respected by their neighbours (1 Timothy 3:2-7; Titus 1:6-7). Gaining the respect of others is a sign that we are maturing spiritually and that we manifest God's nature in our daily lives.

New Christians are often zealous but lacking in wisdom. And our zeal can be offensive to many. But as we mature we learn how to be wise in our zeal. We are not wrong to be zealous. But even Jesus had to grow in wisdom as He grew in age.

Many people became Jews as a consequence of the new decree. The inference in the text is that they were afraid that they might be caught up in the coming killing frenzy. But many would also respond to the miraculous way God had saved His people. This was an obvious miracle which no one could deny. We do not know whether those people made a permanent choice to become Jews or whether they reverted to their original nationality after the threat to their safety declined.

Today, we are at the beginning of a great harvest which will be seen throughout the world as people turn to Jesus for their salvation. There will be many different motives for an individual's decision to turn to Jesus. Some will be caught up in the general enthusiasm and respond emotionally to the call. Others will fear losing friends if they do not follow their lead. Others will want to be part of a loving and caring community, not realising the "cost" of following Jesus. Many of these decisions to turn to Jesus will not be permanent because of the challenges of life. But among those who will not last the course, there will be many who find a genuine relationship with God.

Mordecai had signed the decree. The peoples were celebrating. But, the Jews had not won their battle yet. The day of reckoning was fast approaching when two decrees became operational on the same day. A battle between good and evil was still to be won.

Today, we live in a similar situation. Two spiritual decrees are in operation: the wages of sin is death but the gift of God is eternal life. The battle lines have been drawn. There is always a battle to be faced, some larger than others. We have the decree of God which says that we will go from victory to victory. But we always have to take our place in the battle.

Thirty

Esther 9:1-10 *"So on March 7 the two decrees of the king were put into effect. On that day, the enemies of the Jews had hoped to overpower them, but quite the opposite happened. It was the Jews who overpowered their enemies. The Jews gathered in their cities throughout all the king's provinces to attack anyone who tried to harm them. But no one could make a stand against them, for everyone was afraid of them. And all the nobles of the provinces, the highest officers, the governors, and the royal officials helped the Jews for fear of Mordecai. For Mordecai had been promoted in the king's palace, and his fame spread throughout all the provinces as he became more and more powerful. So the Jews went ahead on the appointed day and struck down their enemies with the sword. They killed and annihilated their enemies and did as they pleased with those who hated them. In the fortress of Susa itself, the Jews killed 500 men. They also killed Parshandatha, Dalphon, Aspatha, Poratha, Adalia, Aridatha, Parmashta, Arisai, Aridai, and Vaizatha— the ten sons of Haman son of Hammedatha, the enemy of the Jews. But they did not take any plunder."*

The 7th March finally arrived, the day on which the two decrees were put into effect. There had been several months of planning by both the Jews and their opponents for this day. But the expected victory of the Agagites and Amalekites was turned into a rout as the Jews overpowered their enemies.

No one could stand against the Jews because everyone was afraid of them. In contrast, the Jews were full of faith, knowing that the Lord was fighting for them. The fear the Jews had felt when the first decree of Haman was passed for their destruction had been swallowed up by the faith released when the Lord obtained the second decree for their defence.

Today, we are still in the conflict between fear and faith. Do we live in fear or in faith? Fear cripples but faith releases. We often have to fight fear in order to enter into faith. I had a personal battle with fear in 2020. It was not the pandemic, Covid-19. That held no fear for me. I was confident that my times are in the hands of the Lord. My struggle came from a small conflict, something which others would deal with without losing any sleep.

Although the issue was insignificant, the enemy used it to cast a shroud of darkness over me. I was in a battle with a spiritual enemy. After a few months, I came through the other end of the tunnel knowing the Lord had given me the victory. But it was a battle I had to fight using the word of the Lord.

If we have had to face a spiritual attack of fear we know what the Agagites and Amalekites felt as they faced the Jews. They were crippled, unable to resist as the Jews defended themselves. Consequently, the Jews destroyed many of their enemies throughout the empire.

In the city of Susa, the city where their enemy had plotted their demise, the Jews slaughtered five hundred men, including the ten sons of Haman. The number ten is often a symbol for man's limited ability. And it is a strangely suitable number for the sons of Haman. In their human strength they sought to destroy God's chosen people. But they only had a limited strength which could not compare with the power and authority of God. They failed. And man will always fail in an attempt to destroy God's people.

Under the decree of Mordecai, the Jews had been given authority to take the property from the people they slaughtered but they did not take that opportunity. Instead, they accepted no reward for their activity on that day.

Many years earlier, Abraham had also refused to accept any plunder from the kings who had kidnapped his nephew Lot (Genesis 14:21-24). His reason was that he wanted nothing from unrighteous people. He did not want to give them an opportunity to allege that he had gained his wealth from them. Although we are not specifically informed this was the reason why the Jews did not take plunder from the Amalekites, it is the probable one.

Today, we can also be tempted to obtain money by "taking plunder". Sometimes, we are offered a devious opportunity which looks good but does not come from God. For example, perhaps we have been abused by someone who has stolen from us. We do not have the right to steal from them in revenge. It is better to wait for the Lord to bring His justice.

God will provide us with money in His way and in His time, often in surprising ways.

Thirty one

Esther 9:11-19 *"That very day, when the king was informed of the number of people killed in the fortress of Susa, he called for Queen Esther. He said, "The Jews have killed 500 men in the fortress of Susa alone, as well as Haman's ten sons. If they have done that here, what has happened in the rest of the provinces? But now, what more do you want? It will be granted to you; tell me and I will do it." Esther responded, "If it please the king, give the Jews in Susa permission to do again tomorrow as they have done today, and let the bodies of Haman's ten sons be impaled on a pole." So the king agreed, and the decree was announced in Susa. And they impaled the bodies of Haman's ten sons. Then the Jews at Susa gathered together on March 8 and killed 300 more men, and again they took no plunder. Meanwhile, the other Jews throughout the king's provinces had gathered together to defend their lives. They gained relief from all their enemies, killing 75,000 of those who hated them. But they did not take any plunder. This was done throughout the provinces on March 7, and on March 8 they rested, celebrating their victory with a day of feasting and gladness. (The Jews at Susa killed their enemies on March 7 and again on March 8, then rested on March 9, making that their day of feasting and gladness.) So to this day, rural Jews living in remote villages celebrate an annual festival and holiday on the appointed day in late winter, when they rejoice and send gifts of food to each other."*

King Xerxes received a report that the Jews had slaughtered five hundred of their enemies in Susa. No report was given of any losses to Israel which suggests there were none. Other than wondering how many had been slain in his empire, the king does not seem to be concerned about the loss of life. Instead, he again invited Esther into his presence and asked if she had any further requests.

Esther did not hesitate, immediately asking for a further day of slaughter. The king readily agreed to her request. Today we tend to be pacifists, hating war. But that is a recent development caused through the horrendous losses accumulated in the world wars of the previous century. The danger is that our pacifist attitudes to physical war reduce our commitment to the spiritual war.

Esther wanted to destroy every physical enemy. Today, we need to be committed to destroy every spiritual enemy. When we win a battle, there are usually survivors which escape because we do not press in to destroy every enemy which has stood against us. We are content to bring down the main obstacle. And having done so we erroneously assume we have finished that particular battle.

The king gave the Jews permission to continue to defend themselves the following day, March 8th and in Susa alone a further three hundred men were killed. In the rest of the empire seventy five thousand Amalekes had been killed on March 7th. No plunder was taken on any day.

Having successfully defended themselves, the Jews celebrated with a day of rest and feasting. In Susa, the celebration was a day after the rest of the empire because there had been two days of fighting in the city.

We have seen the full sequence of emotional responses as the story of Esther has developed. We started with peace in captivity. And perhaps that peace had lulled the Jews into complacency. They did not expect to be threatened by an unknown enemy. Today, we can live in comparative peace and luxury. But we should not become complacent. An enemy can attack us suddenly without warning.

From complacency, the Jews went to fear and mourning, fasting and tearing their clothes in hopelessness. But the faith of Mordecai and Esther was contagious, transforming fear into bold expectation. And when the day of conflict arrived, that faith brought great success, leading to overflowing joy and celebration.

Today, we also can suffer the same fluctuating emotions. We should not be dismayed when we are fearful. Fear provokes us to seek the Lord. And when we seek Him, we will find Him. We will also find His strategy to overcome the enemy. From fear we will move to faith as we take hold of the words and promises of God. And faith will lead us into victory.

If we stay in fear, we should be concerned because we are not living in the peace and rest of God. He promises us His peace as we live in Him. We should not be satisfied until we find Him.

Thirty two

Esther 9:20-26a *"Mordecai recorded these events and sent letters to the Jews near and far, throughout all the provinces of King Xerxes, calling on them to celebrate an annual festival on these two days. He told them to celebrate these days with feasting and gladness and by giving gifts of food to each other and presents to the poor. This would commemorate a time when the Jews gained relief from their enemies, when their sorrow was turned into gladness and their mourning into joy. So the Jews accepted Mordecai's proposal and adopted this annual custom. Haman son of Hammedatha the Agagite, the enemy of the Jews, had plotted to crush and destroy them on the date determined by casting lots (the lots were called purim). But when Esther came before the king, he issued a decree causing Haman's evil plot to backfire, and Haman and his sons were impaled on a sharpened pole. That is why this celebration is called Purim, because it is the ancient word for casting lots."*

Although the text above states that Mordecai recorded the events of the story written down in Esther, it probably refers to the letters he sent to the Jews rather than to the account in the bible. He wrote the account into the letters so that every Jew understood the reason for the celebration of those two days.

As it was only the Jews in Susa who had fought for two days, the Jews in the rest of the empire would not know the full extent of the great victory. Mordecai wanted everyone to understand the fullness of what God had achieved for them.

Mordecai established an annual feast to commemorate the victory. This feast took its place among the other annual feasts of Israel which had been established by Moses and is still commemorated today. It is called "Purim", a name derived from the Persian word meaning "casting lots".

We might think it strange to name a religious feast to commemorate casting lots, particularly with our cultural disapproval of gambling, but the title is full of deeper significance. Haman had put his faith in the lots. He chose the most favourable day to achieve his plan dependent on the lots. Therefore, Purim declares that God is more powerful than the god of the lots.

The name also declares that our times are in God's hands alone. We are not at the mercy of our enemies. We are cared for by God.

As part of the annual celebration, the story of Esther is re-enacted. The need for fasting and prayer is rehearsed before the interventions of Esther and Mordecai are acted out. Gifts of food are given to each other and to the poor. It is a time of feasting and rejoicing.

It is good to remember what God has done for us. We often become so overcome by the challenges we face that we forget how God has helped in the past. But when we remember previous victories, we realise that God is able to do anything. He will deliver us in the present.

The religious feasts such as Easter and Whitsun give some specific opportunity to remember what God has done in a general way. But we need to also remember the specific times He has helped us personally. The day on which we were born again was the start of a fresh journey with God. It is good to remember what we were like before and after that momentous day.

Every challenge we face gives the opportunity to grow with God to see His victory each time. The victory might be a change to our character and attitude or it might be a different success. But, we can acknowledge the work of God in taking us through to the other side whatever the outcome.

When we have successes to remember, they help us to walk in faith through the next challenge we face. The Lord allows the challenges so that we can become more mature and gain promotion in His kingdom. That is the reason that James tells us to greet the challenge with great joy (James 1:2).

Thirty three

Esther 9:26b-28 *"So because of Mordecai's letter and because of what they had experienced, the Jews throughout the realm agreed to inaugurate this tradition and to pass it on to their descendants and to all who became Jews. They declared they would never fail to celebrate these two prescribed days at the appointed time each year. These days would be remembered and kept from generation to generation and celebrated by every family throughout the provinces and cities of the empire. This Festival of Purim would never cease to be celebrated among the Jews, nor would the memory of what happened ever die out among their descendants."*

The Jews agreed with Mordecai to keep an annual feast to commemorate the victory over Haman. When we consider the many times that God has delivered Israel from national crisis, it is surprising that other events in Israel's history were not commemorated in the same way.

Today, we often celebrate events of history. On an individual basis we might remember our birthday and the dates we were engaged and married to our spouse. We might remember the deaths of particularly loved relatives.

There are national holidays and religious feasts, each stirring our memory for some event. But, the story of Esther is significant for the fact that it was a forgotten event which led to the victory over Haman. Mordecai's loyalty to the king averted a disaster which would have shaken the empire but it had been overlooked. God ensured that Mordecai's good deeds were remembered at the right time.

It is also true that Jesus promises that the Holy Spirit will bring to remembrance what we need when we need it (John 14:25-26). If we have heard something from God in the past, even many years previously, He will remind us when we need to remember what He said.

There is a difference between remembering what the Holy Spirit has said to us and celebrating the victories He has given to us. Our memory of the past helps us to succeed in the challenge. Our celebration of victory honours God by acknowledging all He has done. It is a way to publicly thank Him and to honour Him.

Today, many nations celebrate the feasts of Easter and Whitsun not realising that they were originally among the feasts established by Moses for Israel. The nature of the feasts was changed by Emperor Constantine in an attempt to separate his new religion of Christianity from the Jews. And by establishing new feasts, the emperor lost the true meaning of the old. Consequently, many people celebrating the new feasts today do not even acknowledge that God exists.

In the New Testament, there are many letters from Paul to the early Christian communities. The letters were written to expose some of the false doctrines and practices of those groups. And one of the issues Paul raises more than once is keeping feast days. His conclusion is that we cannot earn our salvation by keeping any rituals, including the feasts and there is no obligation from God for us to keep the feasts. We are accepted by God to the measure of our faith in Jesus.

The problem Paul was addressing was that the legalistic Jews insisted that Gentiles and Jews kept the feasts in order to earn God's acceptance. Paul rebuked them for this because keeping the feasts has never been necessary for acceptance by God.

However, Paul does not address the issue of using the feasts to remember God's victories. We do not know what he thought about that issue.

Moses established the feasts to remember certain events and to use them as a reminder of what is to come. Jesus kept the feasts during His earthly ministry. In fact, some of the longer teachings from Jesus were given during the feast of Passover.

I am not suggesting we should religiously keep the feasts each year. But it would be helpful to understand what the feasts commemorated and to develop our personal celebrations to commemorate what God achieves.

Thirty four

Esther 9:29-32 *"Then Queen Esther, the daughter of Abihail, along with Mordecai the Jew, wrote another letter putting the queen's full authority behind Mordecai's letter to establish the Festival of Purim. Letters wishing peace and security were sent to the Jews throughout the 127 provinces of the empire of Xerxes. These letters established the Festival of Purim—an annual celebration of these days at the appointed time, decreed by both Mordecai the Jew and Queen Esther. (The people decided to observe this festival, just as they had decided for themselves and their descendants to establish the times of fasting and mourning.) So the command of Esther confirmed the practices of Purim, and it was all written down in the records."*

Now we read that Queen Esther put the weight of her royal position behind that of Mordecai when she wrote another letter confirming that the new feast of Purim should be accepted by all Jews. We are not told the reason for this royal intrusion into what Mordecai had already agreed. Perhaps there was some disagreement between the Jews in Susa and those in the rest of the Empire over which dates should be celebrated because those in Susa had defended themselves for an extra day.

Apparently, the actual dates for fasting and feasting were decided by the people but traditionally there is usually a day of fasting on the 13th Adar to remember Esther's fast before the feasts of the following two days. Adar is the sixth month of the civil year and the twelfth month of the ecclesiastical year on the Hebrew calendar, roughly corresponding to the month of March in the Gregorian calendar. It is a winter month of 29 days.

The national feasts of Israel commemorate specific events when God delivered His people from their enemies or when a significant milestone was achieved. They usually have some prophetic purpose, encouraging Israel to expect the purposes of God to come to pass. Much of the prophetic symbolism has already been fulfilled through the work of Jesus on the Cross. But there are still future fulfilments for which we are waiting.

The feast of Purim is unusual in that it focuses on the past. Even so, we can receive much from the Lord as we remember the feast. When we remember the faithfulness of God for His people, we can receive His faithfulness for ourselves. When we fast, we can know that God answers our cry to Him. When we feast, we can experience the joy of deliverance from certain death.

There is also much symbolism which reflects the life, death and resurrection of Jesus. Just before His death on the Cross, the disciples of Jesus despaired for Him and for themselves, just as the Jews had lost hope when Haman passed his decree. The death and resurrection of Jesus took place over three days, a time when the disciples lived in fear and confusion, in the same way as the Jews had lived during their time of fasting. But at the resurrection of Jesus the fear and confusion was turned to joy and faith just as it was for the Jews when Mordecai passed his decree.

We also pass through these emotional stages on our daily journey to faith. When a challenge confronts us we do not always immediately respond with faith. Our enemy catches us by surprise, deceiving us to despair at bad news. If we do not realise we are under attack we might need to spend time with God to renew our faith in Him and to receive His peace.

As we listen to the words of the Spirit of God He will restore our souls. He will encourage us to persevere until we have the victory over the challenge we face.

The feast of Purim is a joyful one because it celebrates victory. But we do not have to wait until a feast before we can be joyful. In fact, the Lord encourages us to live in joy. We read that the joy of the Lord is our strength (Nehemiah 8:10). Paul wrote that *"The Kingdom of God is love, joy and peace"*. The fact is that we can be joyful always because we live in the victory of Jesus. He has defeated our enemy already. Our commission is to establish the victory of Jesus in every stronghold which our enemy illegally holds.

Thirty five

Esther 10 *"King Xerxes imposed a tribute throughout his empire, even to the distant coastlands. His great achievements and the full account of the greatness of Mordecai, whom the king had promoted, are recorded in The Book of the History of the Kings of Media and Persia. Mordecai the Jew became the prime minister, with authority next to that of King Xerxes himself. He was very great among the Jews, who held him in high esteem, because he continued to work for the good of his people and to speak up for the welfare of all their descendants."*

As we come to the end of the story of Esther, the author ties up a few loose ends.

There does not seem to be any immediate relevance to the fact that King Xerxes imposed a tax throughout his empire other than it balanced out his earlier generosity when he crowned Esther as his queen. We have already seen that the king was controlled by his emotions. It is possible that the slaughter of the Amalekites gave him reason to be concerned about the state of the finances of the Empire.

However, the fact that the author writes about the great achievements of Xerxes suggests that the taxation was necessary to enable those deeds, whatever they were. We were informed earlier that he built large palaces. He also spent money on other buildings. But his largest costs were in the constant battles against the Greeks.

Compared to Xerxes, the great deeds of Mordecai are clearer. Although the records of the Medes and Persians which relate to him have not been found to this date, the author wants us to acknowledge how Mordecai was a caring Prime Minister as he looked after the administration of the Empire.

The fact that the author speaks about the memory of Xerxes and Mordecai indicates that it was neither of these who wrote the biblical account. Much like many of the biblical books, the account could have been written many years after the events. But the rigid control of the story-telling communities would ensure the validity and honesty of the story.

The two contrasting obituaries of Xerxes and Mordecai might cause us to wonder how others will record our lives. To some extent it does not matter what others think of us because we live to serve God alone. The only opinion that matters is what He decides about our lives.

Having said that, however, if we testify to knowing God, what others think of us determines what they think of Him. Do we demonstrate a character like Xerxes or like Mordecai? Are we controlled by our emotions or by the Spirit of God? Are we men and women of faith or of fear?

The story of Esther shows us that there is nowhere in the world where we do not have access to God. Even though the Jews were in captivity and a long way from Jerusalem, the Lord heard their cries for help. It is the same for us today. We might have wandered far from God. We might be in "captivity" to many things. But God can and will deliver us.

Other publications by John J Sweetman
Paperback and EBooks:
The Book of Genesis trilogy:
    Part One: The Beginnings
    Part Two: Abraham and Isaac
    Part Three: Jacob and Joseph
Establishing the Kingdom series:
    The Book of Joshua
    The Book of Judges
    The Book of Ruth
    The Book of 1 Samuel
    The Book of 2 Samuel
The Book of Romans
The Book of 1 Corinthians
The Book of 2 Corinthians
The Book of Galatians
The Book of Revelation
The Emerging Kingdom
Babylon or Jerusalem – your choice

Recommended Book by Fiona Sweetman – Paperback and EBook

    Taste the Colour Smell the Number

Any feedback, questions or other communication with John Sweetman is possible through email:

jsweetman77@outlook.com

Printed in Great Britain
by Amazon